Head Vases E
The Artistry of Betty Lou Nichols

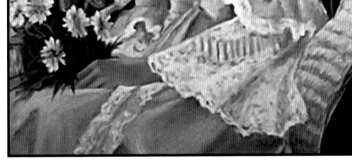

Maddy Gordon

Schiffer Publishing Ltd ®

4880 Lower Valley Road, Atglen, PA 19310 USA

Library of Congress Cataloging-in-Publication Data

Gordon, Maddy.
Head vases, etc. : the artistry of Betty Lou Nichols / by Maddy Gordon.
p. cm.
ISBN 0-7643-1490-4
1. Nichols, Betty Lou--Catalogs. 2. Head vase planters--Collectors and collecting--California--Catalogs. 3. Pottery--
20th century--Collectors and collecting--California--Catalogs. I. Title.
NK4210.N428 A4 2002
738.8--dc21
2001004850

Designed by Bonnie M. Hensley
Cover design by Bruce M. Waters
Type set in VivaldiD/Zapf Humanist BT

ISBN: 0-7643-1490-4
Printed in China
1 2 3 4

Published by Schiffer Publishing Ltd.
4880 Lower Valley Road
Atglen, PA 19310
Phone: (610) 593-1777; Fax: (610) 593-2002
E-mail: Schifferbk@aol.com
Please visit our web site catalog at **www.schifferbooks.com**
We are always looking for people to write books on new and related subjects.
If you have an idea for a book, please contact us at the above address.

This book may be purchased from the publisher. Include $3.95 for shipping.
Please try your bookstore first. You may write for a free catalog.

In Europe, Schiffer books are distributed by
Bushwood Books
6 Marksbury Avenue
Kew Gardens
Surrey TW9 4JF England
Phone: 44 (0) 20 8392 8585
Fax: 44 (0) 20 8392 9876; E-mail: Bushwd@aol.com
Free postage in the UK. Europe: air mail at cost.

Dedication

I dedicate this book to Luanne Nichols Shoup, beloved daughter of Betty Lou Nichols. Her knowledge, passion, and appreciation of her mother's work have made this book possible, and her boundless enthusiasm and encouragement have been my inspiration.

Acknowledgments

No book is the work of just one person, especially a book of this nature. Without the help, support and cooperation of countless individuals, this book could not have been written. I wish to express my appreciation to Peter Schiffer of Schiffer Publishing Ltd. for accepting my proposal for this book and to my editor (and new best friend) Donna Baker.

I am especially grateful to the family and friends of the late Betty Lou Nichols. They opened their homes and their hearts and shared their memories and their collections. Luanne Nichols Shoup and her husband Michael took photography courses to assist in photographing the family's collection. In fact, they became so proficient that they began second careers as photographers. In addition, Luanne studied ceramic restoration in order to repair all her mother's work before photographing it, and she is now also involved in that line of work.

John Nichols, Betty Lou's husband, was a tremendous help. He furnished me with old catalogs, brochures, newspaper articles, and other materials that he had accumulated over the years. Without those materials, this book couldn't have been as accurate or complete.

Other family members and friends who shared their memories and collections included Betty Lou Nichols' son, Michael Nichols, Betty Lou's brother and sister in-law, Don and Jackie Renken, Stanley and Barbara Olsen (who worked in the original factory), John's sister, Virginia Moiola, and friends Shirley and Harold Muckenthaler, Dixie Chamberlin, and Boe Holiday.

Warm and heartfelt thanks to Mike Posgay and Ian Warner who helped to pique my interest in Betty Lou Nichols with the informative section they wrote about her in their book *The World of Head Vase Planters*. They also generously shared their personal correspondence with Ms. Nichols. To the best of their and my knowledge the information published in their book was the first documented record of that talented artist.

I am grateful to Jan Fontes and George Alig who opened their charming shop, "The Antiques Gallery" (Fullerton, California), early one Sunday so that my husband, Bruce, and I could photograph their extensive collection.

My sincere thanks to the many people who sent me photographs to be included in this book. Special thanks to Debbie Clint of Los Angeles who not only allowed me to photograph her collection but also invited other collectors to bring their pieces to her home, thereby saving my traveling to their several homes. For the last two years Debbie also has sent me a steady stream of pictures as she has added to her already superlative collection.

Others who sent in pictures include: Margot Banke, Pam Corbin, David Davidson, Moshe Dahan, Mary Ensslin, Edith E. Fairbanks, Garth Auctions (Delaware, Ohio), Bonnie Griffith, Ethel Horne, Judy Kegler, Lauren Kest, John and Diane Leach, Dale Luger, Diane Luger, Bruce L. Lytle, Vannoye Maestrejuan, Charles and Joyce H. Neal, Juvelyn Nickel, Jose Ortiz, Carolyn Smith Paschal, Art and Betty Potash, Peggy Powell, Jean Rich, Linda M. Strzesynski, Bob and Clara Sweet, Jennifer Sykes, Eleanor Vlack, Carole Watkins, Earl Watson, Frances Finch Webb, Kay Williams, Ruth Worthington, and Nanette Canepa Zupon.

Special thanks to Maureen Antash and the whole staff of Advance Photolab of Scarsdale, New York for their skill and endless patience. I wish to express my gratitude to Ann Staib whose decoding skills enabled her to make sense out of my nearly illegible handwriting and type this manuscript.

Thanks to all the dealers (Barry Schmuecker, Mike Nickel, Dord Johnson, etc. etc.) and collectors who helped me to build my collection. My sincere apologies to anyone that should have been mentioned but was inadvertently omitted. Last but not least I want to thank my husband, Bruce, who for thirty-six years of our marriage has been a constant source of support and encouragement in all my endeavors.

Contents

Pricing Information _____ vi

Our Mother, Betty Lou Nichols _____ 7

Biography _____ 8

Identification and Price Guide _____ 17

    The Flora-Dorables _____ 17

    The Young Adorables _____ 65

    The Egg Heads _____ 68

    The Demi-Dorables _____ 72

    One-of-a-Kind (So Far) _____ 73

    The Figurines _____ 76

    The People Bottle Line _____ 104

    Betty Lou's Adorable Animal World _____ 108

    The Christmas Line _____ 117

    Plates and Mugs _____ 128

    Unique Items _____ 130

    Miscellaneous Items _____ 131

    The Paintings _____ 136

Original Catalog Brochures _____ 143

The Marks _____ 159

Bibliography _____ 160

Pricing Information

A price guide is just that – a guide. The prices in this book are my "guesstimate" of what a serious collector might be willing to pay for a piece in excellent condition.

A definitive value for any one piece does not exist. Supply and demand, condition, size and scarcity all help determine the value of a piece. Prices have been known to vary greatly depending on geographic location as well the forum in which the merchandise is being sold – garage or tag sale, flea market, antique show or shop, on the Internet, etc. In addition, dealers might charge somewhat more than a collector selling a duplicate piece will.

As with any collectible, the selling price is predicated in large part on the condition of the item (damage and repairs). Because of the fragile nature of Betty Lou Nichols' ceramics, i.e., the delicate ribbons, lashes, bows, and hair curls that have painstakingly been added by hand to the original molds, her work has been particularly subject to damage through the years. For this reason collectors find that they have to accept deviation from perfection in order to fill out their collections. The more scarce the piece, the more willing is the collector to accept a damaged piece. Likewise, a moderate amount of light crazing, so common in many of the California ceramics, is quite acceptable. Dark or brown crazing is definitely less desirable.

A mint specimen, almost impossible to find, might command more than the prices listed in this book while a damaged piece will probably sell for considerably less, depending on the severity of the damage. Regarding repairs, it is often difficult for the collector to determine whether a piece has been subject to repair. For this reason, the buyer must beware.

Hopefully, the accompanying price guide will help the collector compare the relative value of one piece to another. In the final analysis, a sale is made at the price at which a willing buyer and a willing seller meet.

Our Mother, Betty Lou Nichols

By Luanne Nichols Shoup

My mom was a woman with a tremendous amount of energy and creativity. She had a lot of friends, but she was really a family person. Both my parents were. She was raised in a Christian home and kept her belief in Christ to the end. Many Sundays for twenty-five years the family met at church and had breakfast together.

Mom and Dad were married for over fifty years. Mom appreciated nature. She loved birds, trees, and fish. She liked to swim and snorkel. Later in life, while snorkeling in Hawaii with her grandsons, she would recite the names of every fish. She and my dad also took the boys to any place that had birds – zoos, aviaries, etc. She had a great sense of humor and a low threshold for boredom. She loved every form of art. Although she was known for her ceramics and painting, she was also an excellent seamstress.

Her favorite place was our cabin in the San Bernardino Mountains. This is where we had some of our best moments. When I was very young, she had me painting alongside of her, giving me guidance on mixing colors and composition. We would go on long walks, taking photographs of trees and rivers to paint on canvas.

As an adult, some of my favorite memories are during the winter months at the cabin when it snowed. We would go out at the first sign of daylight and spend hours taking photographs and enjoying the fresh snow sparkling in the sunlight. These were our best of times, creating art and enjoying God's perfect design.

Betty Lou Nichols and her daughter Luanne, then six years old. Note Florabelle head vase and small figurines behind it.

The multitalented Betty Lou Nichols was born Betty Louise Renken on November 22, 1922. Right from the beginning most everybody called her B'Lou (pronounced "blue"). She was a direct descendant, on her mother's side, of Arthur Middleton, one of the signers of the Declaration of Independence. Her mother's family was from Texas, her father's from Iowa. Her parents settled in Southern California, where she was born and raised. Betty Lou grew up to be a very in touch person who saw and appreciated the beauty all around her. She spent her life translating it into various art forms. Her life was guided by this insatiable desire to create beautiful things. "I have never wanted to do anything else. It has always been art for me," Betty Lou was once quoted as saying. Therefore, when Miss Reeder, Betty Lou's seventh grade teacher, first encouraged her to make art her lifetime career, this advice fell on receptive ears.

Award ribbons from the 1935 and 1936 California State Fairs.

Always drawing and painting, Betty Lou won the first prize ribbons for her work at California State fairs in 1935 and 1936, while still in junior high school. From 1936 to 1940, Betty Lou attended Fullerton High School (where in 1997 she was posthumously inducted into the Fullerton High Hall of Fame). It was during her high school years that Betty Lou became acquainted with ceramics. She intended to eventually become an art teacher because she felt that was really about the only career in the arts open to women.

Betty Lou Nichols at six years old.

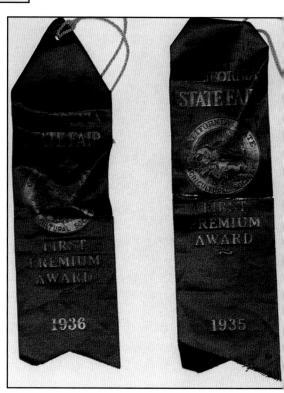

Plaque from Fullerton High School Wall of Fame.

Always sketching and drawing, she was the artist for her college newspaper, the *Torch*, and for her college yearbook. When offered a scholarship to Chanards Art College in Los Angeles (quite an honor during World War II), Betty Lou chose instead to marry her college beau, handsome engineering student, John Nichols. They were married in April of 1943 in her parents' home.

Betty Lou attended Fullerton Junior College from 1940 to 1942, where she was an art major. Her teacher, Lucille Hinkel, further encouraged her painting. Also, it was at Fullerton Junior College that Betty Lou studied under Mrs. Mary Hodgedon, who was considered the foremost authority on ceramic work in California. This is where Betty Lou really developed her talents as a ceramist. Early, one-of-a-kind pieces from that period were signed "Betty Lou Renken."

Betty Lou and John Nichols.

"I Wonder What Kind Of A Bicycle He Drives?"

Drawings from her college newspaper (1942).

When Betty Lou and John met, John was attending Fullerton Junior College during the day and working evenings and summers at Volte. Volte made aircraft and John worked there on the sheet metal assembly for the airplanes.

After their marriage, John, who was in the army, was sent to Texas for basic training. There, Betty Lou got her first job working as a photographer's assistant. Her job was to color the black and white photos. She would take the pictures and line them up on the bed. Then she would take the pink and do all the cheeks. After that, she would take their lip color and paint the lips. She had her own little assembly line, a forerunner of her later ceramic ventures. She did quite well during this period. When John was relocated to Stockton, California – where a lot of the men were stationed before being shipped out – Betty Lou got a job as a photographer (she actually took the pictures) and portrait finisher. She did so well that she made more money then many of the high-ranking officers in the military.

As long as John was stateside, Betty Lou would follow him to the various military bases. When, however, John Nichols was posted overseas with the 13th armored division in January of 1945, Betty Lou returned to California and moved into her parents' home at 118 West Frances Avenue in La Habra. As Betty Lou wrote in a letter to Mike Posgay and Ian Warner (authors of The World of Head Vase Planters) dated November 9, 1989: "All through the 1930's we had been in what was known as the Great Depression. There certainly was no extra money for frills. When the war started, the men went to war and the women went to work. Of course, there were no imports from Germany, Japan, or Italy and the English were busy just staying alive. It was a classic case of being in the right place at the right time with the right thing."

It was at this time in 1945 that Betty Lou gave birth to her son, Michael, and that same year Betty Lou Nichols Ceramics was born in her parents' backyard, at the site of her old playhouse, with a one cubic foot gas kiln. This kiln could handle five pieces of pottery at a time. As Mike Posgay and Ian Warner wrote "… the first figures Betty Lou made were called 'The Gay 90s.' She started out with casting plain cone skirt, bust and head. Then her innovation was to roll out the modeling clay quite thin with a rolling pin, cut it in strips and make ruffles for skirts, curls for hair etc. She had experimented with this technique of using clay like fabric while still in school and liked the feel of it." This technique soon became the hallmark of Betty Lou Nichols' products and is an easy way for today's collectors to recognize a Nichols piece.

Betty Lou in her parents' backyard with her early Gay '90s figurines.

Betty Lou's first customer was Bullock's Department Store in Los Angeles. The downtown Los Angeles Bullock's was "the place to shop" and Betty Lou used to dream that someday her creations would be in their window. Her brother Don drove her over there with a box of "little dollies" – her Gay '90s figurines. Bullock's bought them all and ordered more – this was her first commission. When she got that order she was still working with her one cubic foot kiln. Additional orders soon followed. Betty Lou's pieces sold so well that she had to hire someone to help her with the painting. Eventually, she employed four or five artists who brought their lunches with them to work and played bridge during the lunch hour. They remember Betty Lou as a wonderful person to work for – enthusiastic and fair with a great sense of humor. "She was a darling – we all loved her," remembered Stan and Barbara Olsen. Stan worked on the molds and Barbara was one of the artists. Stan made $200 a month as a salaried worker, while Barbara and the other artists were piece workers at 25 cents apiece. They did quite well. Barbara saved enough to buy a new car, quite a feat at that time.

Betty Lou's goal was to become as good and successful as Kay Finch, who was already becoming a creative force in the development of Southern California's ceramic industry. Kay was almost twenty years older than Betty Lou. Ironically, however, a few years later Betty Lou Nichols and Kay Finch would share the same sales representative – Ruth Sloan.

Ruth Sloan's Los Angeles showroom in the early forties, displaying Betty Lou Nichols' and Kay Finch's work. *Courtesy Frances Finch Webb.*

Betty Lou Nichols Ceramics was in full swing when John Nichols returned from overseas. John went to work with Standard Oil and, at the same time, Betty Lou Nichols Ceramics began a period of expansion. They got rid of the playhouse – gave it to a neighbor's child – and built a studio for the artists to work in. Betty Lou and John rented another house just behind her parents' house, built a bigger room for the casting, and got an eight cubic foot gas kiln. Betty Lou's first sales representative was Dillion and Wills, who had been importers before the war. When the war was over, Dillion and Wills went back to importing. However, they introduced Betty Lou to Ruth Sloan, who later became her new representative. Ruth was an experienced sales representative with a keen sense of business. She suggested that Betty Lou come up with something that could display just a few flowers. Fresh flowers were the florist's biggest expense – especially in the winter. At that time, florists had to pay cash every day for their flowers. Ruth's suggestion was the birth of the Betty Lou Nichols' head vases, which have become so popular with today's collectors. The florists loved them and so did the public. The Flora-Dorables, as the head vases were called, be-

came a hit item across the country and Betty Lou Nichols Ceramics had to move to even larger quarters.

In 1949, Betty Lou Nichols Ceramics bought a factory at 639 Central Street, La Habra and relocated the flourishing company there. John Nichols left Standard Oil to run the business. Stan Olsen was hired as production manager. Betty Lou's dad, Michael Renken, had been a field-drilling superintendent for Standard Oil, which put him right in sync with installing the gas lines needed for the kilns. John, who had studied engineering in college, built a very sophisticated casting system. There was a large mixing tank with pipes running over the casting tables. Long pressurized air hoses were connected to the pipes with off/on valves at the end so workers could easily fill the molds with the slip. At its peak production, Betty Lou Nichols Ceramics had about thirty employees and two thirty-two cubic foot gas kilns. These large kilns had doors on either end with a loading cart on heavy metal tracks. That way, they could unload and load one cart while the other was firing. They fired a load every twenty-four hours. The company also had two eight cubic foot top loaders for smaller firing and gold firing.

The factory at Central Street in La Habra.

Betty Lou designed the original models. These were then reduced to a base that could be cast in a mold. The cast base was then trimmed, adding ruffles, curls, hats, eyelashes, lace, etc. A mold maker was kept busy full time making molds and castings. Subsequently, the mold making was jobbed out to reduce soaring costs. Translating Betty Lou's original creations into a plaster mold, which comprised as many as two to ten parts, was an exacting task and a vital one.

Since they had to keep all the pieces wet while working on them, they built a wet room. This was a room about 8' x 12' with plaster of Paris slabs on the shelves which were kept wet all the time. Four to five different kinds of clay coming from as far away as Kentucky and Tennessee, plus other additives, were blended with a big mixer in a 250-gallon redwood tank. The resulting slip was cast in molds and dumped when the correct thickness adhered to the mold. These bases were then stored in the wet room until a modeler could finish them by adding eyelashes, hats, ruffles, etc. using white modeling clay. The pieces were then put back in the wet room to wait for a painter. Barbara Olsen, wife of the production manager, was one of the painters. The "paint" was clay-based slip with color stain that was ball milled on the premises.

To make the eyelashes, ruffles, and other details, they would roll out the modeling clay with a wooden rolling pin on a damp cloth. The eyelashes were added to the pieces by hand; consequently they vary in length and appearance. The eyelashes are unique in that no one else did eyelashes like Betty Lou's. Putting soft clay through a pasta machine made the spaghetti, which is found on the Santas. The zig zag edges found on hats and ruffles were created with a pasta cutter. Bric-a-brac found on Judy, Jill, Polly, and Becky was dipped in slip and applied to the bodice. Lace and mesh fabrics were also dipped in slip and attached to the more elegant ladies, as in Stephanie's shawl and Melissa's dress. All parts had to be kept damp or they wouldn't adhere. When painting, everything had to be damp to get a nice smooth finish. After all the modeling and painting was finished and the piece was completely dry, it was fired twice at about 1800° degrees. The first firing resulted in the bisque piece, which was then dipped in glaze and fired the second time. If gold was required, a third firing at a lower temperature was needed. The ready mixed glazes were purchased from Wards.

At the very beginning of production Betty Lou would sign "B'Lou" on all the pieces. As the business grew she changed this to "Betty Lou Nichols." She also had whichever artist painted the piece sign for her and then initial the signature so Betty Lou could look back and see who did it if any errors had to be corrected. However, Betty Lou would paint all the lips herself, as she was very particular about the lips and the cheeks and wanted them to look uniform. The pink lip and cheek colors were hers alone – nobody else ever used these colors.

The heads and most of the figurines were named on the bottom of the pieces. On occasion, however, a piece slipped out unsigned or with the wrong name due to human error.

In 1950, John and Betty Lou moved to their new home in Fullerton, California, where John still lives. That same year Betty Lou gave birth to their daughter, Luanne. Betty Lou later designed two head vases named after Luanne, which are some of the head vases most sought after by collectors. With the exception of the Madonna, Luanne is the only head vase with a full upper bodice and hands. When Luanne was about eight years old, she took ballet lessons. This inspired Betty Lou to design four wall pocket ballet girls also named Luanne.

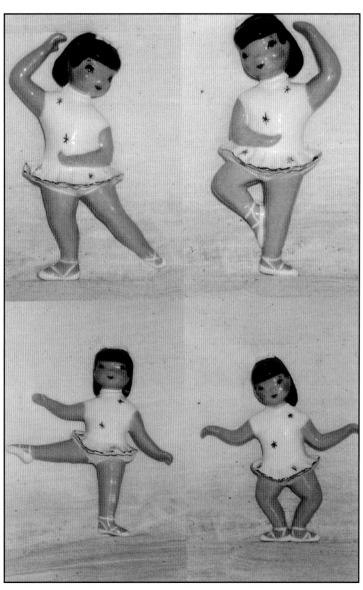

Wall pocket ballet girls named for Betty Lou's daughter Luanne.

Some of Betty Lou's pieces were named after friends, cartoon characters, and famous people. Some names were picked just because they were funny – like the two egg-heads, Eggbert and Henrietta. Henrietta was one of the cartoon characters Betty Lou created while she was attending Fullerton College. Ermyntrude was named after the ermines on her dresses; Mary Lou was named after the first artist to work for Betty Lou Nichols Ceramics; Tom and Becky were from the "Tom Sawyer" story. Among the Dixiebelles, Virginia was named after John's sister (Betty Lou's sister-in-law and close friend). Among the Ready Reindeer, one is named Sam, after a close family friend who smoked cigars.

In the summers, when Luanne and her brother Mike were older, they would do quite a bit of the casting. They sometimes got into clay fights while waiting for the slip to set up. One of the tools Luanne liked to play with was her mom's throwing machine. John had made this with a treadle sewing machine using an axle and bearing from an old Ford pickup he got at a junkyard. He then poured a plaster of Paris base on top of the axle. Betty Lou liked this wheel because she could control the speed with her feet.

The Gay '90s figurines and head vases were followed by a "pleasant peasant" line, plates and mugs, decanters, and a variety of other flower holders, figurines, and giftware items. Along with the early Gay '90s pieces and some other items – such as the angels, ducks, bunnies, and peasants – the artists were given free reign with the added modeling and painting, giving those pieces a wide variation in their appearance. As production increased and as cost efficiency became important, Betty Lou established a standard pattern for her employees to follow.

Among the work done for different clients were figurines produced for the Walt Disney Company (from the film *Fantasia*). These characters were produced for a very short period of time; consequently, only about six hundred were made. They are very rare and difficult to find, and since they do not have Betty Lou Nichols Ceramics marks on them, very few people know of this production line.

Betty Lou also took special orders, which explains the personalized items and the occasional different design. Centennial Sue, for example, was designed for a special centennial in the state of Colorado. Some organizations would order a particular item, such as one of the bottle people, and have

their group name put on it. Betty Lou even personalized cups and other items with the names of family and friends.

Betty Lou Nichols Ceramics had a retail store in front of the factory where they sold "seconds." A second was a piece that was considered inferior. Some of the defects could be the paint not covering evenly, a broken or bent tip on a hat bow, or a piece that might crack during the firing. Although the seconds were sold then at a discount, they seem to bring as high a price as regular quality pieces in today's market. The presence of a factory outlet explains why even though the company had national and worldwide distribution, many more pieces seem to be available in Southern California. On a more humorous note, John Nichols remembers a lady coming into the shop and picking up a piece and blowing into it. When asked why she was doing this she said the piece said "blow" under it. Actually it said B'Lou of course, but she thought it said blow.

Business was slowing down after a while with Ruth Sloan, so Betty Lou engaged a new representative by the name of W.A. Curie, Inc. The head vases were not selling all that well at this point. Curie had many contacts, however, and encouraged Betty Lou to come up with new figurines. This resulted in the production of a line of elegant ladies, including Stephanie, Angela, Melissa, Felice, Madelon, and more. Curie told Betty Lou that if they would start a Christmas line in the summer, he would purchase everything they could produce. Curie also gave Betty Lou Nichols Ceramics a $10,000 advance to cover the production cost of the Christmas line.

Making the head vases was great while it lasted, but there was unfortunately no such thing as a design copyright to protect the artists' work. The end of the war marked the beginning of the end of most of the Southern Califor-

John Nichols examining the "seconds" in the retail shop.

nia potteries. The Japanese copied almost everything Betty Lou designed. They copied her head vases and called them the Francis heads. Due to cheap labor and low overhead, copies were often produced at half the price of the originals. Although the quality of the copies was not equal to that of Betty Lou's pieces, demand for her work began to fall off. In an effort to retain business, Betty Lou turned to the production of figurines for the Walt Disney Company and the production of jam and syrup containers for Knotts Berry Farm – the oldest independent amusement park in the country. This was unfortunately not enough to save her company and Betty Lou Nichols Ceramics went out of business on November 22, 1962, Betty Lou's fortieth birthday. "I can remember Mom struggling with the idea of closing her doors, and her and my dad having long discussions on what decision to make." remembers Luanne. "After all, this was her passion. I will never forget that early, cold, dark November morning when my mom, my brother and I drove the last order to Knotts Berry Farm in her station wagon. My brother was in high school by then and very strong, so he did most of the unloading. I

can still hear my mom say 'That's it' after everything was unloaded, and the slamming shut of the tailgate on our station wagon."

While one door closed, another opened. Gradually, the lure of brush and canvas absorbed her time and interest as Betty Lou turned to painting. She was internationally known for her work in ceramics, and, in a short time, she began gaining recognition for her character studies and landscapes. She turned to painting full time.

As a native of California, Betty Lou was particularly interested in the people of the early West. She made an extensive study of the Indians and Mexicans and their customs. Her favorite portrait subjects were children and the elderly – the former because of the innocence and wonder in their continuing discoveries of life around them, the latter because life had deeply etched character lines in their faces, which told an intriguing story on canvas. Two of her commissions included a portrait of Mrs. Walter Knotts, which can still be found on display at the Knotts Berry Farm, and a portrait of Dr. William T. Boyce, Fullerton College's first President, which still hangs in the college library.

Portrait of Mrs. Walter Knotts, which still hangs at Knotts Berry Farm.

Betty Lou Nichols at forty – but she wasn't smiling the day that she had to close the business.

Dr. William T. Boyce's portrait from the Fullerton Junior College Library.

Betty Lou became very well known locally as a painter. In fact, she was soon better known as a painter than as a ceramist. She was chairman of the Muckenthaler Cultural Center in Fullerton, where she arranged the monthly art exhibit, and also taught painting privately in her studio. Eventually, she became very well known as an artist in both California and Arizona. At one time, a successful developer in Scottsdale, Arizona named Calvin Wolfswingle was buying just about everything Betty Lou painted. He would place one of her paintings in each house he had for sale.

Betty Lou had many successful gallery shows in Scottsdale and Phoenix, Arizona, and Palm Springs, San Diego, and Fullerton California, as well as in many other area galleries. Most of the paintings done for the public she signed B.L. Nichols, because at the time Betty Lou felt women were not respected as painters. However, when the paintings were made for family members and close friends, she did sign her full name: Betty Lou Nichols. In January of 1994, Betty Lou sold her last and largest

Landscapes were another favorite of this artist. Betty Lou felt that she was most fortunate to live in the southwest because there was so much material at her fingertips: the ocean and rivers, the majestic mountain ranges of California, and the unending beauty of Arizona. She particularly enjoyed autumn on the desert. She visited Arizona regularly and took photos to bring home to translate into oil paintings in her studios. She was not an enthusiastic field painter, preferring the comfort of working in her studio.

A friend of the family, a Dr. McClelland, would go to the Navajo reservations every year to fit the Indians with free eyeglasses. He was always inviting Betty Lou and John to join him, and one summer they did. Normally reclusive, the Indians accepted Betty Lou since she was a friend of the doctor. Betty Lou took many photographs and brought them home to portray in oil on canvas.

A recent photo of John Nichols and Luanne Nichols Shoup outside the Fullerton home.

painting for $1400 to a friend who had just built a new home in California and wanted an important piece for her entryway. Shortly thereafter, Betty Lou suffered from the first of two strokes and passed away on August 6, 1995 at the age of seventy-three, just as the popularity of her ceramic head vases began resurfacing. "She would have gotten a big kick out of all this," said her husband, John Nichols, who still lives in their Fullerton home.

Betty Lou with her last and largest painting in January 1994.

The Flora-Dorables

Betty Lou made most of the head vases in the Gay '90s style because the hats of that period were very large and heavily decorated with feathers and flowers – which, according to Betty Lou were really fun to craft. All these head vases have closed eyes and lack eyebrows, as Betty Lou felt that eyebrows would be a distraction and she wanted to keep the faces simple. This is another of her trademarks, along with her eyelashes, curls, and ruffles.

Florabelle

Florabelle, the largest head vase produced by the Betty Lou Nichols Ceramics Company, measures approximately 11". Since the eyelashes, curls, bows, and ruffles were made from clay and individually applied to the body of the heads, there is some variation in the height of these heads. Because the hats were individually affixed to the heads, there are also differences in the brims of the hats, from relatively flat to curved – sometimes almost approaching the shape of a cowboy hat. While Florabelle was probably the only Betty Lou head vase that was made in just one size, it was made in more colors than any other head. Its large size made it relatively easy to paint and encouraged experimentation with different color combinations. Catalogues from 1950 and 1952 show that the wholesale price of Florabelle was $8.75. Today many of these vases sell for one hundred times that price.

The features that distinguish one Florabelle from another (and often affect the prices) include: the beauty and scarcity of the color combinations; the size and artistic appeal of the hats, particularly the brims; the size and configuration of the bows; the extent of the ruffles on the front of the dress; and the length and lateral extent of the eyelashes.

Plate 1. Florabelle 11". With auburn hair, which is somewhat less common than blond or black haired Florabelles. Note the three layers of the ruffles instead of usual two on this magnificent head. Estimated value: $1500.

Plate 2

Plate 3

Plate 4

Plates 2 to 4. Florabelle 11 ½″. Three different views of Florabelle with very desirable color combination and magnificent bow. Estimated value: $1500.

Above: Plate 5. Florabelle 12". Bow repaired. Estimated value: $1000.
Top right: Plate 6. Florabelle 11". Estimated value: $1100.
Bottom right: Plate 7. Florabelle 11 ½". Estimated value: $1000.

Plate 8. Florabelle
11 ½". Estimated
value: $1100.

Left: Plate 9. Florabelle 11". Full ruffles reach almost shoulder-to-shoulder, huge hat. Estimated value: $1300.

Right: Plate 10. Florabelle 12". Estimated value: $1200.

Left: Plate 11. Florabelle 11 ½". Estimated value: $1200.

Right: Plate 12. Florabelle 10 ¾". Very narrow ruffles just in center of dress. Estimated value $900.

20

Left: Plate 13. Florabelle 11". Estimated value: $1000.

Right: Plate 14. Florabelle 11". Estimated value $900.

Left: Plate 15. Florabelle 13". Scarce - only one known where undercoat and (one) ruffle are black. Estimated value: $1500.

Right: Plate 16. Florabelle 11 ¼". Estimated value $1100.

21

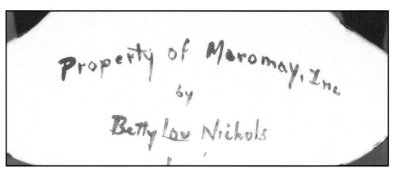

Plate 18. Bottom of personalized Florabelle from Plate 17.

Plate 20. Florabelle 12". Note very curved hat brim, eyelashes reach almost to hair. Estimated value: $1300.

Plate 17. Florabelle 11". Special order. Personalized hat reads "Party for you" in French. Estimated value: $1400.

Plate 21. Florabelle 10 ¾". Note very flat brim on hat. Common color combination, small eyebrows, small ruffles. Estimated value: $800.

Plate 19. Florabelle 11". Estimated value: $1100.

Plate 22. Florabelle 11". Estimated value: $1000.

Plate 23. Florabelle 11 ½".
Estimated value: $900.

Plate 24. Florabelle 12". Scarce - only one known made in just two colors. Estimated value: $1300.

Plate 25. Florabelle 11". Estimated value: $1100.

Plate 26. Florabelle 11". Hat looks a little small for head. Estimated value: $1000.

Plate 27. Florabelle 11 ½". Estimated value: $1300.

Plate 28. Florabelle 11". With rare polka dotted outfit. The artists preferred painting polka dots, as they were the easiest to do. Estimated value: $1500.

Plate 29. Florabelle 10 ¾", 10 ¾". Both show the most commonly found color combination. The florists loved the green and yellow colors – they felt those colors went very well with fresh flowers. Estimated value: $800 each.

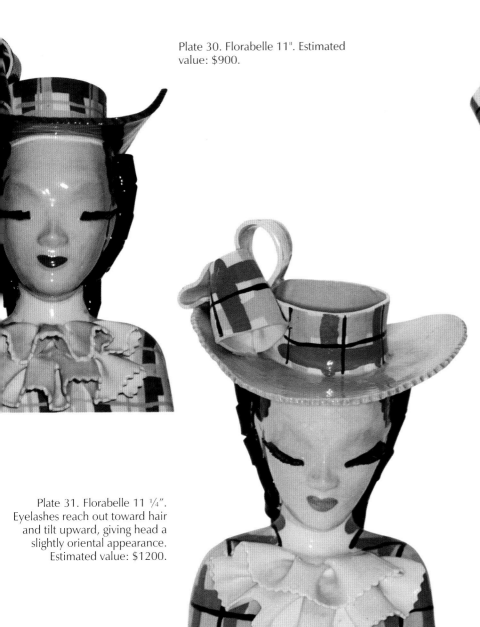

Plate 30. Florabelle 11". Estimated value: $900.

Plate 32. Florabelle 11". Estimated value $900.

Plate 31. Florabelle 11 ¼". Eyelashes reach out toward hair and tilt upward, giving head a slightly oriental appearance. Estimated value: $1200.

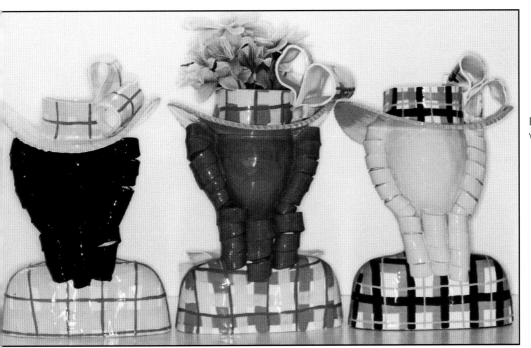

Plate 33. Back view of Florabelle with three hair colors.

25

Plate 34

Plate 35

Plates 34 and 35. Rare 9 ½" heads are marked Florabelle although they are unlike any Florabelle we have ever seen. Estimated value: $2000.

The Florabelle Lamps

A woman used to come to the factory to purchase Florabelles. She made them into lamps for resale. It appears they were all placed on the same black bases and outfitted with elaborate shades. This typically doubled the height of the heads. Estimated value: $1600 each.

Plate 39

Plate 36

Plate 40

Plate 37

Plate 38

Plate 41

27

Ermyntrude

Ermyntrude is one of the most popular of Betty Lou Nichols' head vases. It comes in two sizes – approximately 6" and 8". The original catalog price was $6.25 for the 8" head and $3.75 for the 6" head. Ermyntrude also comes in five beautiful colors. In increasing order of scarcity, they are two shades of green, yellow, white, and pink. The furs were applied by hand to the bodies by several different artists, so they were often applied in different positions, as were the hats. Occasionally an Ermyntrude will have the name Yvonne on the bottom.

Plate 44. Ermyntrude 8 ½", 6". Estimated value: $500, $250.

Plate 42. Ermyntrude 8", 6". Estimated value: $600, $300.

Plate 45. Ermyntrude 8 ½", 6 ½". Emerald green with three stripes. Estimated value: $650, $350.

Plate 43. Ermyntrude 8", 6". Estimated value: $650, $350.

Plate 47. Ermyntrude 6". Does not usually have blond hair. Estimated value: $450.

Plate 48. Ermyntrude 6". Solid green dress. Estimated value: $350.

Plate 46. Ermyntrude 8". Rare pink color. Estimated value: $900.

Plate 50

Plates 49 & 50. Ermyntrude 6", and Japanese copy 5". Estimated value: $300, $65.

Plate 49

Plate 51. Ermyntrude 7 ¾", 6". It was not until later years that the puffed sleeve and cape effect were incorporated into the design. Earlier models had rounded shoulders. Also note fur in the center of dress rather than on shoulder. Estimated value: $700, $400.

Luanne

This beautiful vase was named after Betty Lou Nichols' daughter and is quite unusual. While most head vases are just head and shoulders, this figure is really a "bust." Besides Luanne, only the Madonnas are busts with hands. Luanne comes in two sizes, 10" and 9", two styles, tuxedo front and ruffled collar, and several different color combinations.

Plate 53. Luanne 9". Estimated value: $1300.

Plate 52. Luanne 9". Rare dress design. Estimated value: $1500.

Plate 54. Luanne 9". Estimated value: $1200.

Plate 55. Luanne 10", 9". Estimated value: $1200 each.

Plate 57. Luanne 10". Estimated value: $1200.

Plate 56. Luanne 9 ½". Estimated value: $1200.

Plate 58. Luanne 10 ½". Somewhat scarce tuxedo front.
Estimated value: $1400.

Mary Lou

Mary Lou was named after the first girl to work for Betty Lou Nichols Ceramics. The head vases she painted can be identified by the initial M on the bottom. There appear to be three styles named Mary Lou.

Plate 59. Mary Lou 8", 5 ½". Estimated value: $500, $200.

Plate 60. Mary Lou 8", 6". Less common later version incorporated puffed sleeves into the design. Estimated value: $600, $300.

Plate 61

Plates 61 & 62. Mary Lou "officially" comes in two sizes, 8" and 6", but in these photos the range is from 5" to 9".

Plate 62

Plate 63. Mary Lou 9". Note rare ruffled front on this Mary Lou (similar to that of Florabelle). Estimated value: $650.

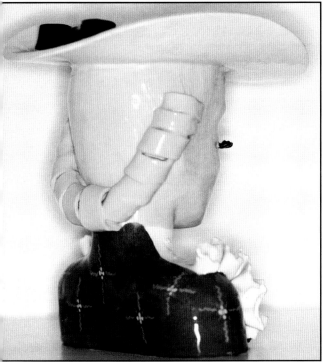

Plate 64. Mary Lou 8". Purple dress. Estimated value: $550.

Plate 65. Mary Lou 8". Rare plaid dress. Estimated value: $600.

Plates 66 to 68. Mary Lou 8", 6". Three views. Estimated value: $800, $400.

Plate 66

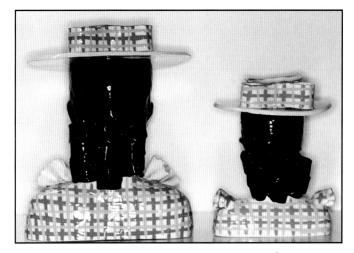

Plate 67

Plate 68

Plate 69

Plate 70

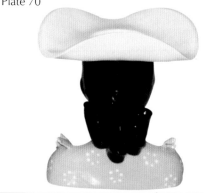

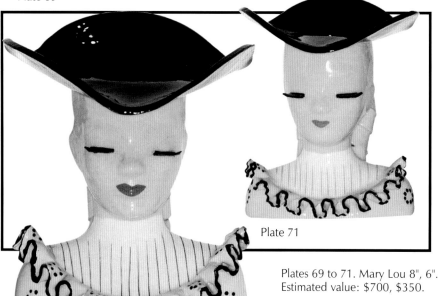

Plate 71

Plates 69 to 71. Mary Lou 8", 6".
Estimated value: $700, $350.

Plate 73. Side view of Plate 72.

Plate 72. Mary Lou 8". Note size differences
in white under blouse and brown necklace.
Estimated value: $700 each.

Vicky

All the Vickys have a cape incorporated into their dress design.

Plate 74. Vicky 9 ½ ".
Estimated value: $800.

Plate 75. Vicky 6 ½" each.
Estimated value: $400 each.

Plate 76. Vicky 8", 6". Estimated value:
$800, $450.

Plate 77. Vicky 8", 6".
Estimated value: $800, $450.

Plate 78. Vicky 8", 6"
("Snowflake" Vicky).
Estimated value:
$800, $400.

Plate 80

Plate 79

Plates 79 & 80. Vicky 6", copy 5 ½".
Estimated value: $400, $60.

Plate 81

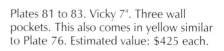

Plate 82

Plates 81 to 83. Vicky 7". Three wall
pockets. This also comes in yellow similar
to Plate 76. Estimated value: $425 each.

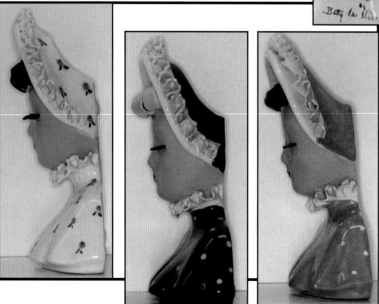

Plate 83

36

Nellie

Plate 84. Nellie 8", 6". Estimated value: $800, $400.

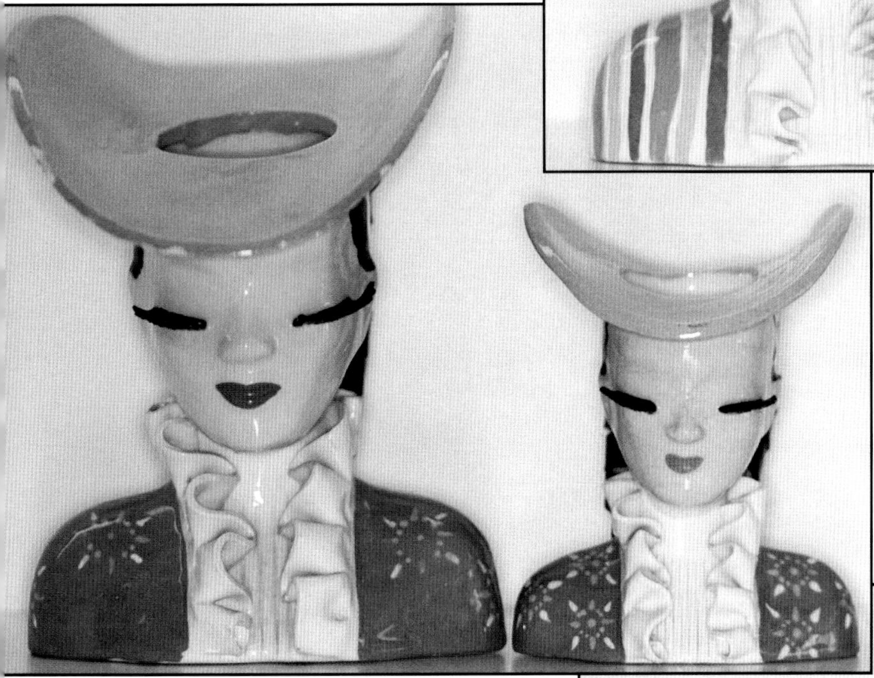

Plate 85. Nellie 8", 5 ½ ". Estimated value: $750, $375.

Plate 86. Nellie, Miss Nellie 6", 8". Estimated value: $400, $800.

Plate 87. Nellie 8". Estimated value: $800.

Plate 88. Nellie 6". Estimated
value: $400.

Plate 89

Plates 89 & 90. Nellie 9".
Estimated value: $800.

Plate 90

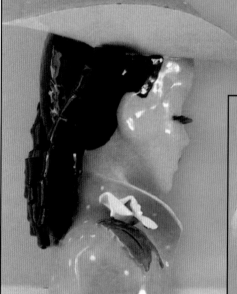

Plate 91. Nellie 8 ½", 6". Estimated
value: $750, $350.

Plate 92. Nellie 8 ½", 6". Estimated value: $750, $350.

Plate 93. Nellie 8 ½", 6". Estimated value: $750, $350.

Plate 94. Nellie 6". Estimated value: $300.

Plate 95

Plates 95 to 97. Nellie copy, Nichols' Nellie. Estimated value: $55, $350.

Plate 97

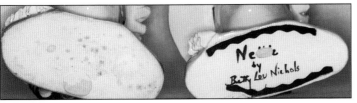

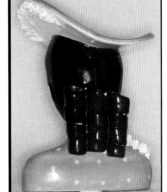

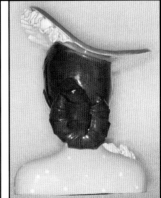

Plate 96

Nancy Lou and Nancy

Plate 98. Nancy Lou 8". Estimated value: $500; Nancy 6". Estimated value: $300.

Plate 99. Nancy Lou 8". Estimated value: $600.

Plate 100. Nancy 8", 6". Note ruffled front. Estimated value: $600, $350.

Plate 101. Nancy 6", 8", 6". With more common dress. Estimated value: $300, $650, $300.

Plate 102. Nancy 8", 6".
Estimated value: $750, $350.

Plate 103. Nancy 8", 6". Note unusual hat brim on left bent up, on right turned down. Estimated value: $950, $350.

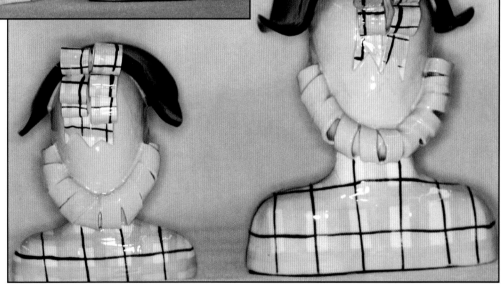

Plate 104. Nancy 6", 8". Estimated value: $350, $950.

Plate 105. Nancy 8". Unusual colors.
Estimated value: $850.

Linda

Plate 106. Linda 8", 6".
Estimated value: $700, $350.

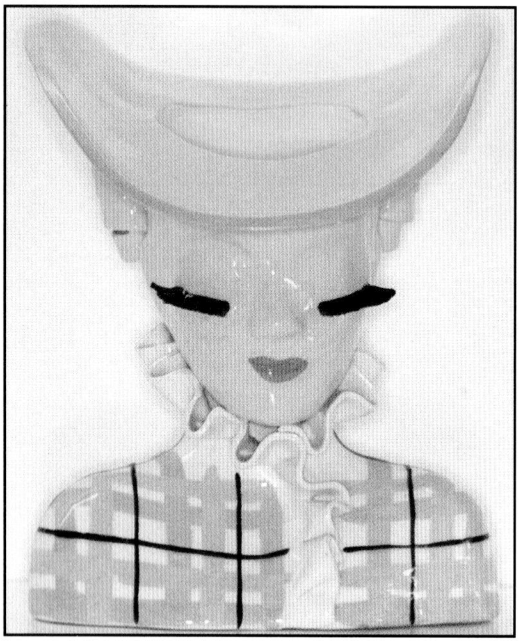

Plate 107. Linda 8". Estimated value: $700.

Plate 108. Linda 8". Estimated value: $750.

Plate 109. Linda 8". Estimated value: $750.

Plate 110. Linda 8". Estimated value: $750.

Plate 112. Linda 8". Estimated value: $700.

Plate 111. Linda 8", 6". Estimated value: $700, $350.

Plate 113. Linda 6". Estimated value: $350.

43

Plate 114. Linda 5 ¾", 7 ½".
Estimated value: $400, $800.

Plate 115. Linda 8 ½", 5 ½". Estimated
value: $800, $400.

Plate 116. Linda 8".
Estimated value: $850.

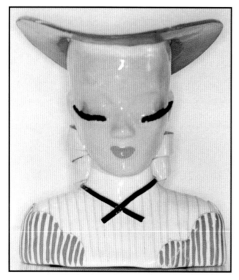

Plate 117. Linda 8". Estimated value:
$850.

Plate 118. Linda 8".
Estimated value: $850.

Plate 119. Linda 8". Estimated value: $850.

44

Valerie

Plate 120. Valerie 5" to 9".

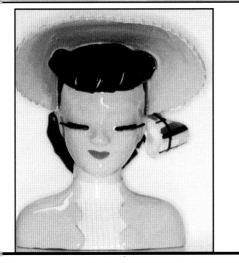

Plate 121. Valerie 8", 6".
Estimated value: $650,
$350.

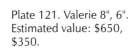

Plate 122. Valerie 6 ¾", 8".
Estimated value: $350, $650.

Plate 123. Four small Valeries
5 ¾" to 6 ¾". All four
probably come in 8". Estimated value: $350 each.

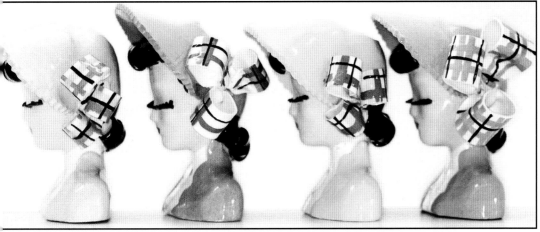

Plate 124. Side view. Note
differences in hats and bows.

Plate 125. 8 ½" nicknamed "The Valentine Valerie." Estimated value: $900.

Plate 126. Valerie 8". Estimated value: $850.

Plate 127. Valerie 8". Estimated value: $850.

Plate 128

Plates 128 & 129. Valerie 8". Estimated value: $850.

Plate 130. Valerie 8". Estimated value: $850.

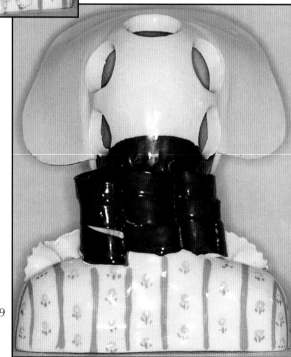

Plate 129

46

Plates 131 & 132. Valerie 8", 6".
Estimated value: $850, $450.

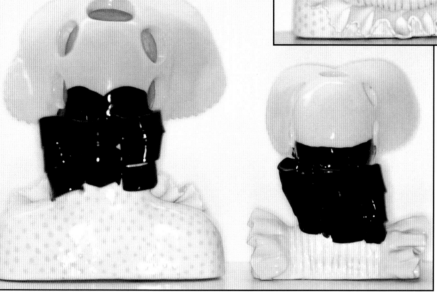

Plate 131

Plate 132

Plate 133.
"Valentine"
Valeries 8", 6".
Estimated value:
$900, $500, pair
$1500.

Plate 134. Three small (6") Valeries. Estimated value: $450 each.
Probably all three have large head vases to match.

Plate 135. Valerie 8", 6". Estimated value: $800, $400.

Plate 136. Valerie 6", 8". Estimated value: $400, $800.

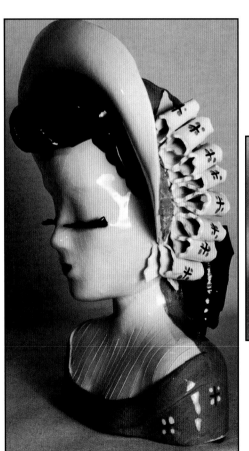

Plate 138. Valerie copy 5 ¾", Nichols' Valerie 6". Estimated value: $60, $400.

Plate 137. Valerie 8" side view.

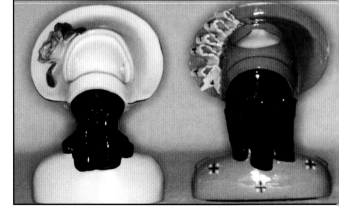

Miss Bows and Buttons

Plate 139

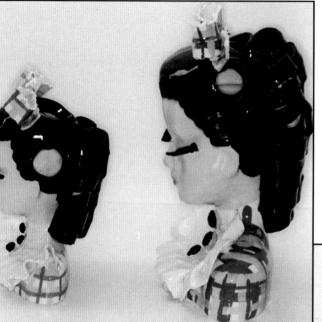

Plates 139 to 141. Miss Bows and Buttons. Three views of this exceptionally beautiful head vase 8", 6". Estimated value: $1000, $500.

Plate 140

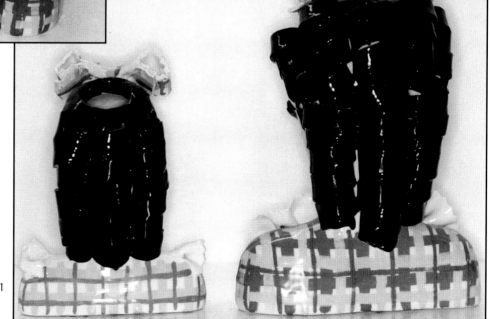

Plate 141

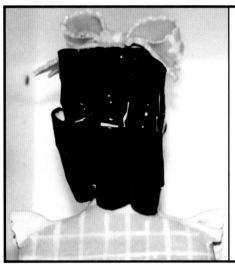

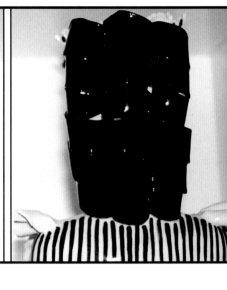

Plate 143

Plates 142 & 143. Miss Bows and Buttons 6", 6". Estimated value: $500 each.

Plate 142

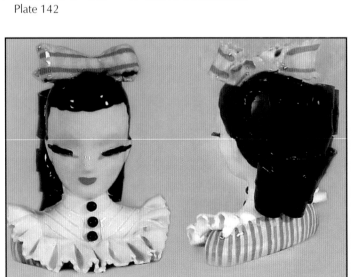

Plate 146. Miss Bows and Buttons 6". Estimated value: $500.

Plate 144

Plate 145

Plates 144 & 145. Miss Bows and Buttons 8", 6". Estimated value: $1000, $500.

Louisa

Plate 147. Louisa 6 ¾″ high, very wide (7 ½″) 5 ¾″ puffed shoulder vase. Estimated value: $650, $325.

Plate 148. Louisa copies 8″, 6″. Estimated value: $65, $40.

Plate 149. Bottom of Nichols' Louisa and copy, 6″ each.

The Scarce "Skinny Neck" Girls

These include Lili, Mitzy, Anna, and Nanette (also Colette and Suzanne who are in the catalog pages but haven't appeared yet). All come in 9" and 7".

Plates 150 to 152. Lili 9 ½". Scarce. Estimated value: $1500. This head also comes in 7". Estimated value: $750.

Plate 150

Plate 151

Plate 152

52

Plate 153. Mitzi 7 ½". Scarce.
Estimated value: $750.

Plate 154. Anna 9", 7". Scarce.
Estimated value: $1500, $750.

Plate 155. Nanette 9". Only one
known so far. Estimated value: $1900.

Michelle, Candy, Cynthia

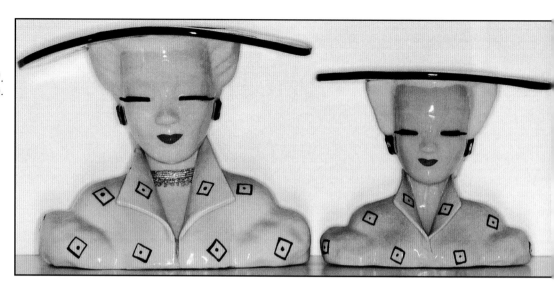

Plate 156. Michelle 8", 6".
Estimated value: $700, $350.

Plate 157. Michelle 6",
copy 6". Estimated value:
$300, $55.

Plate 158. Michelle 6". Unusual color
for Michelle. Estimated value: $400.

Plate 159. Candy 8", 6". Estimated value: $700, $350.

Plate 160. Candy 8", 6". Estimated value: $700. $350.

Plate 161. Cynthia 8", 6". Both colors come in both sizes. Estimated value: 8" pink, very scarce, $1200; 8" white, scarce, $950; 6" $425 each.

Centennial Sue and Sue

Plate 162. Centennial Sue 8". Special order for the Colorado State Centennial. Estimated value: $900. Sue 6". Estimated value: $450.

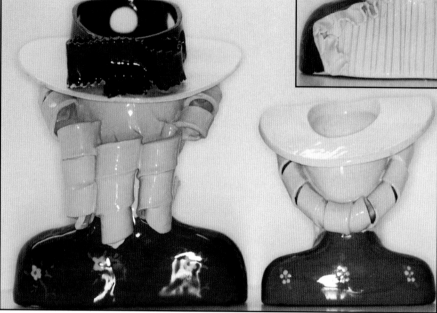

Plate 163. Rear view of Centennial Sue and Sue.

Plate 164. Sue 6". Estimated value: $450.

Plate 165. Sue 8", 6". Estimated value: $700, $350.

Sunny Lou and Miriam Lou

There were a limited number of the Sunny Lous made because the crimped hats proved somewhat fragile.

Plate 166. Sunny Lou 8", 6".
Estimated value: $1500, $650.

Plate 167. Back view, showing complicated hat designs.

Plates 168 & 169. Miriam Lou 6", 8". Estimated value: $400, $750.

Plate 168

Plate 169

Plate 170. Miriam Lou 6". Estimated value: $400.

The "Madonnas Beautiful" Head Vase Planters

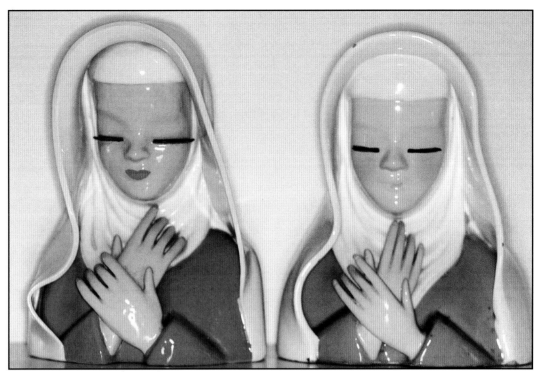

Plate 171. Nichols' Blue Madonna 9", Japanese copy 9". Estimated value: $100, $45.

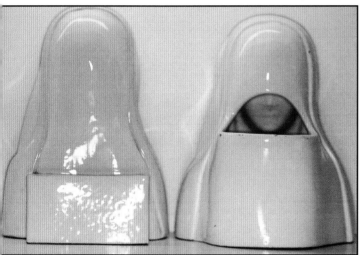

Plate 172. Back view of Plate 171. On all Nichols Madonna planters the planter part was made separately, then attached to the head. All copies have the opening for the plants incorporated into the mold.

Plate 173. The three sizes (9", 7", 4") and styles of the Nichols Madonna. 4" slightly less commonly found than larger ones. Estimated value: $75, $65, $85.

The Spanish Ladies
All three of the Spanish ladies are scarce and all come in 8" and 6".

Plate 174. Rosita 8". Estimated value: $1100 (6", not shown. Estimated value: $575).

Plate 175. Lita 8". Estimated value: $1100 (6". Estimated value: $575).

Plate 176. Maria 6". Estimated value: $575 (8". Estimated value: $1100).

Plate 177. The three Japanese copies, Juanita, Conchita, and Rosita 5 ¾". Estimated value: $65, $65, $65.

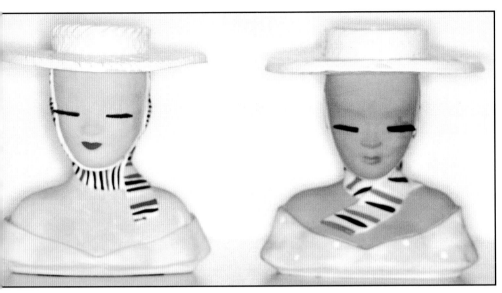

Plate 178

Plates 178 & 179. Nichols' Maria and copy Conchita. Estimated value: $575, $65.

Plate 179

Sheila and Miss Aloha

Plate 180. Sheila 6", 8". Estimated value: $450, $950.

Plate 181. Sheila 6". Estimated value: $400.

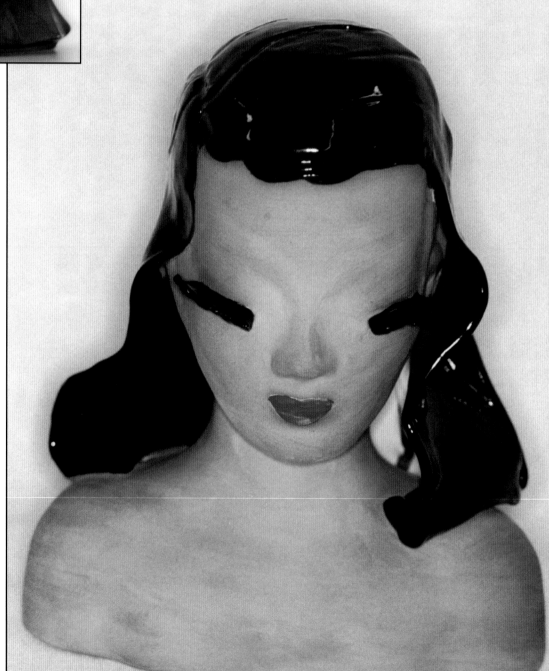

Plate 182. Miss Aloha 8".
Rare Hawaiian head vase.
One of a very few terra
cotta heads – only two Miss
Alohas known so far.
Estimated value: $1900.

Heads Marked Only Betty Lou or Betty Lou Nichols

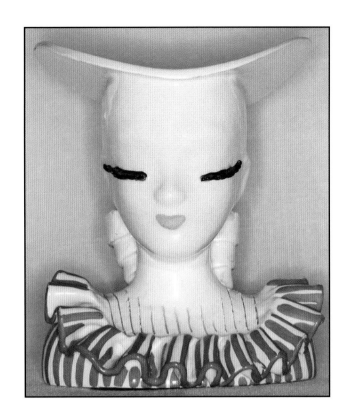

Plate 185. 5 ¼". Estimated value: $350.

Plate 183. 6". Estimated value: $350.

Plate 186. 5 ½". Estimated value: $350.

Plate 184. 6". Estimated value: $350.

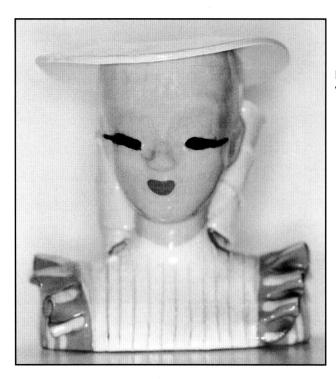

Plate 187. 5". Estimated
value: $350.

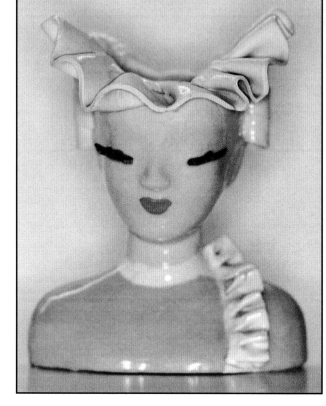

Plate 188. 5 ½". Crimped hat, difficult to find in good
condition. Estimated value: $450.

Plate 189. 6 ¾". One of the very few head
vases without a hat. Estimated value: $450.

The Young Adorables

In contrast to all the other head vases, the Young Adorables have open eyes. Betty Lou painted all the eyes herself to ensure consistency. These heads come in only one size (approximately 5"-6").

Plate 190. All four heads marked Judy, #3 named after Judy Garland, #4 head sometimes marked Polly. 5 ½", 5", 5 ½", 5". Estimated value: $350, $375, $375, $350.

Plate 191. Two heads marked Polly 6", 5 ½". Estimated value: $350 each.

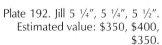

Plate 192. Jill 5 ¼", 5 ¼", 5 ½". Estimated value: $350, $400, $350.

Plate 193

Plates 193 & 194. Kathy 5 ½″, 5 ½″.
Estimated value: $350 each.

Plate 194

Plate 195. Fairy
Queen. Rare. This
was made
especially for
Nichols' daughter
Luanne. It is not
known whether
others exist.
Estimated value:
$1000.

Plate 196.
Becky 6″, 6″.
Estimated
value: $350
each.

Plate 197. Peter 5 ½". Somewhat scarce. It was felt that he looked too much like a girl so production was somewhat limited. Also comes with closed head. Estimated value: $500.

Plate 198. Tom 6 ½". From Tom Sawyer. Estimated value: $375 each.

Plate 199. Becky and Tom from Tom Sawyer. Pair in matched colors. Estimated value: $850 each pair.

The Egg Heads

The Egg Heads come in the very scarce 9" size (Eggbert and Henrietta) and the very common 5" size.

Plate 200. Henrietta 9". Very scarce. Estimated value: $1500.

Plate 203. Eggbert and Henrietta 9", 9". Estimated value: $1800, $1500.

Plate 201. Eggbert 9". Very scarce. Estimated value: $1800.

Plate 202. Eggbert and Henrietta 9", 9". Estimated value: $1800, $1500.

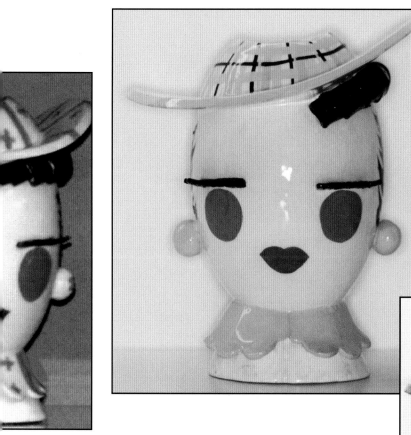

Plate 204. Henrietta 9". Estimated value: $1500.

Plate 205. Henrietta 9". Estimated value: $1500.

Plate 206. Henrietta in the middle of two small eggheads. Estimated value: $75, $1500, $75.

Plate 207

Plates 207 to 211. Small (approximately 5")
matching egghead couples. Estimated value
for a pair: $150.

Plate 210

Plate 208

Plate 211

Plate 209

Plate 212. Small female egghead 5".
Approximate value: $50.

Plate 213. Nichols' egghead (left) 4 ¾", Japanese copy 4 ¾".
Approximate value: $50, $20.

Plate 214. Nichols' small female egghead, Japanese copy. Estimated value: $50, $20.

Plate 215. Bottoms of the Nichols' (far left and far right) and copy (two middle) egg heads. Nichols' eggheads were ink stamped Betty Lou Nichols, La Habra, California. Often this stamp is faded or missing. Dark numbers on bottom of Japanese copies can usually still be found.

The Demi-Dorables

Plate 216. These little 3" heads come in an infinite variety of finishes. The women are more common than the men and closed eyes are more common than open eyes. The estimated value of the women is $75, and the men $100. Open eyes and holiday attire are worth approximately $85 each (note three different shoulder styles on women).

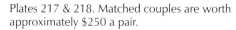

Plate 217

Plates 217 & 218. Matched couples are worth approximately $250 a pair.

Plate 219. Copy and Nichols' head. Approximate value $35, $100.

Plate 218

Plate 220. Nichols' heads are usually hand stamped on bottom, sometimes now faded. Japanese dark numbers are almost always visible.

One of a Kind (So Far)

Only one of these very rare heads has surfaced so far, and none of them appear on any of the original catalog pages. Although they were made from a mold, quite possibly they were not put into production, or at most were made in extremely limited numbers.

Plate 221. Cindy 7 3/8".
Estimated value: $1000.

Plate 222. Donna 5". Estimated value: $750.

Plate 223. 10 ½" Magnificent Florabelle with huge feather instead of bow on hat. The feather proved very fragile so it was not put into mass production. Estimated value: $2500.

Plate 224

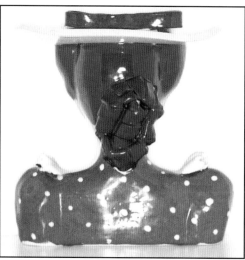

Plate 225

Plates 224 & 225. Mary Lou 6". Very rare Mary Lou that hardly resembles the Mary Lous we are familiar with. Estimated value: $750.

Plate 226. "Removable hat egg head" lady 7 ½". Very few made of this rare head. Estimated value: $800.

Plate 227

Plates 227 & 228. Rare head marked "SAMPLE" on bottom. Perhaps salesmen didn't choose this one or perhaps applied black trim proved to be difficult to apply. Estimated value: $1000.

Plate 228

Plate 229

Plates 229 & 230. Geisha Girl 9 ½". Extremely rare and quite different from other Betty Lou heads (note eyebrows and back of dress). This piece turned up in an estate sale of gentleman who used to work as a janitor for Betty Lou Nichols Ceramics. Betty Lou gave it to him as a gift. Estimated value: $3000.

Plate 230

The Figurines

The Gay Ninety Figurines

The prototypes of the Gay '90s Ladies can be seen at the beginning of these photos. They were one-of-a-kind. They do not have their faces painted on yet because they were still in development. You can, however, see the similarity between these and the later productions. I cannot presume to assign a value for these one-of-a-kind pieces, which are all still in the hands of the immediate family.

Plate 233

Plate 231. 6" Lady with umbrella.

Plate 234

Plates 233 & 234. 5" Lady with umbrella.

Plate 232. 4". Betty Lou made this as a bridesmaid gift for her sister in-law Virginia while studying ceramics at Fullerton Junior College.

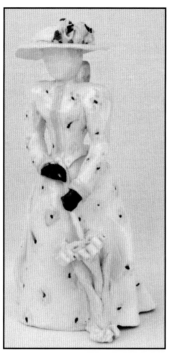

Plate 237

Plate 237 & 238. 6" Winter Lady, dressed for the cold. No others were made like her. Notice the hand is lifting the skirt and exposing her ruffled slip.

Plate 238

Plate 235. 5". Notice the texture in her skirt. Betty Lou was experimenting by rolling her clay on fabric to get a fabric texture.

Plate 236. 5" Lady with umbrella.

Plate 241. 6" Gay '90s Lady and 6" original design.

Plate 240. 6" Flower Lady. A variation of this original design was later put into mass production (see Plate 241).

Plate 239. 6" Dressed for the ball. A similar design was later used for mass production.

Plate 242. This photo shows the development of the Gay '90s figurines.

Plates 243 to 271. Now we get to the Gay '90s Ladies that were mass produced. These 6" figurines were the first production line made by Betty Lou Nichols Ceramics. Betty Lou started with a plain cone skirt, bust, and head. Then her innovation was to roll out the modeling clay quite thin with a rolling pin and cut it into strips for the hair, hat, bows, etc. This was the first line sold to the public and Bullock's Department Store in Los Angeles was the first customer. The figures were not named but are marked "B'Lou" on the inside of the skirt. They were painted however the artists desired, hence the endless colors and styles of these ladies. Very few are alike with the exception of the bride and groom. Estimated value: $350 to $450 each.

Plate 243

Plate 244

Plate 245

Plate 246

Plate 247

Plate 248

Plate 249

Plate 250

Plate 251

Plate 252

Plate 253

Plate 254

Plate 255

Plate 256

Plate 257

Plate 258

Plate 259

Plate 260

Plate 261

Plate 262

Plate 263

Plate 264

Plate 265

Plate 266

Plate 267

Plate 268

Plate 269

Plate 270

Plate 271

Plate 272

Plate 273

Plate 274

Plate 275

Plates 272 & 273. The Brides 6". The Brides were Gay '90s figurines holding bouquets of flowers. Estimated value: $450.

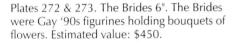

Plates 276 & 277. 6" and 6 ½" Gay '90s couples. The men are very scarce. Estimated value: Women $400, Men $550.

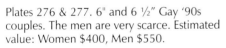

Plate 275

Plates 274 & 275. Brides and Groom 6", 6 ¼". Grooms are extremely scarce. Estimated value: Brides $450, Grooms $600.

Plate 276

Plate 277

The Large Gay Nineties Figurines and Lamps

These approximately 13 ½" figurines were often made with an opening in the bustle and later fitted out at the factory with the hardware necessary for a lamp.

Plate 278

Plates 278 to 288. The 13" to 14" lamps. Those ladies holding floral bouquets were designated "Bridal Lamps" (similar to the small 6" bridal figurines). The parents of Barbara Olsen (who worked in the factory) were friendly with Richard Nixon's family. When Barbara's mom went on a visit "back East" she took one of these large figurines to the White House as a gift for Mamie Eisenhower. After the guards took it to be examines, it was passed along to Mrs. Eisenhower. I wonder where it is now? Estimated value of these large figurines: $1500.

Plate 280

Plate 279

Plate 281

Plate 282

Plate 283

Plate 284

Plate 285

Plate 286

Plate 287

Plate 288

82

Plates 289 to 291. Gay Nineties Lady Lamp 13". This one used to be at the home of Betty Lou's mother on the night stand. John Nichols was going to throw her away because she was broken. Betty Lou said "No don't you dare. I'll be famous some day." Luanne Shoup repaired it and it now stands in her living room.

Plate 289

Plate 290

Plate 291

Plate 292. Figurine 14". Not a lamp. Estimated value: $1500.

Plate 293. Madonna 13". One of a kind, made for Betty Lou's mother. Estimated value: $2500.

Plate 294. 13" Figurine "Mozelle." Estimated value: $1500.

Plate 295. 13" Figurine "Suzanne." Estimated value: $1500.

Plate 296. Two Suzannes and Mozelle.

Plate 297. 13" Figurine "Corrine."
Estimated value: $1500.

Plates 298 & 299. 13"
Figurines. Estimated
value: $1500.

Plate 298   Plate 299

9" Figurines

Plate 300. 9" Adele. Estimated value: $1000.

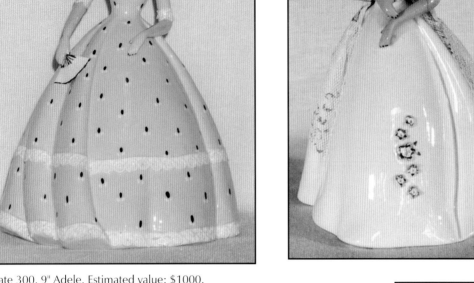

Plate 302. 9" Stephanie. Her shawl was mesh fabric dipped in glaze before firing. The actual fabric would burn out during the firing, leaving the pattern of fabric on the glaze. Estimated value: $1000.

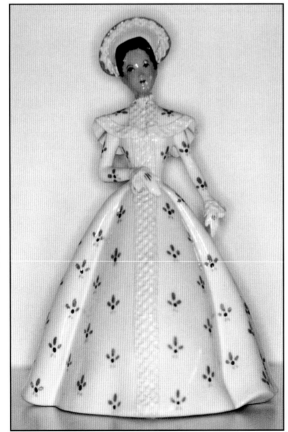

Plate 301. 9" Virginia. Estimated value: $1000.

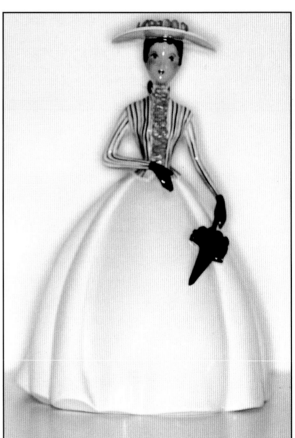

Plate 303. 9" Belinda. Estimated value: $1000.

Plate 304. 9" Angela. Estimated value: $1000.

Plate 305. 9" Rosalyn. Estimated value: $1000.

Plate 306. 9"
Melissa. Lace
was dipped in
glaze before
firing to create
the same effect
as on Stephanie
(Plate 302).
Estimated
value: $1000.

Plate 307. 9"
Jessica. Estimated
value: $1000.

7" Figurines

Plate 308. 7" Madelon. Estimated value: $750.

Plate 310. 7" Laurie. Estimated value: $750.

Plate 311. 7" Becky. Estimated value: $750.

Plate 309. 7" Millicent. Estimated value: $750.

Mothers and Daughters

Plate 312. Mrs. Smith 8", 8".
Estimated value: $75 each.
Suzy 5". Estimated value: $50.

Right & bottom right:
Plate 315. Mrs. Jones
8", Jenny 5". Estimated
value: $75, $50.

Plate 313. Suzy 5".
Estimated value: $50.
Mrs. Smith 8".
Estimated value: $75.

Below: Plate 314. Jenny 5".
Estimated value: $50. Mrs.
Jones 8". Estimated value:
$75. Jenny 5". Estimated
value: $50.

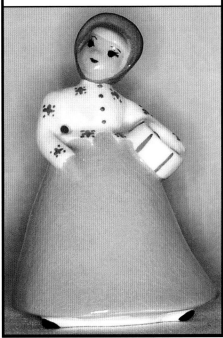

The Dixiebelles

The Betty Lou Nichols Dixiebelles represent the epitome of her ceramic artistry.

Plate 316

Plate 317

Plates 316 & 317. Virginia 10". The skirt is 9" wide. Estimated value: $2500.

Plate 318. Georgia 10". Estimated value: $2500.

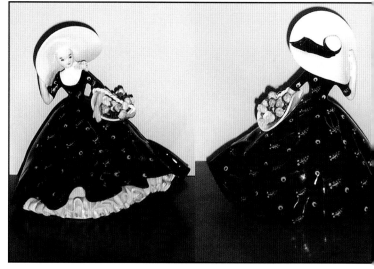

Plate 319. Georgia 10". Estimated value: $2500.

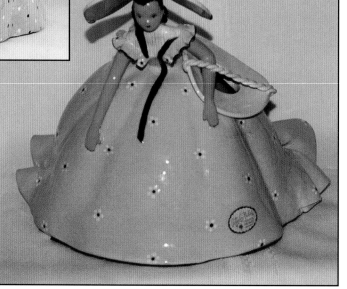

Plate 320. Carolina 10". Estimated value: $2500.

The Pleasant Peasant Series

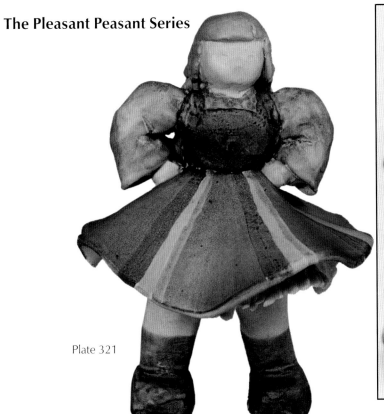

Plate 321

Plate 323. Lisa 10". Estimated value: $200.
Chris 11". Estimated value: $150.

Plates 321 & 322. 7 ½". First design for
peasant girl. No painted face yet. One of a
kind, made at Fullerton Junior College.

Plate 322

Plate 324. Tina with Cart 5 ½". Estimated value: $250.
Tony with Cart 5 ½". Scarce. Estimated value: $350.

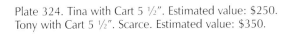

Plate 325. Fritz with Barrel 9 ½".
Estimated value: $85. Anna (Fat
Momma) 9". Estimated value: $85.

Plate 326. Gossip Plaque – Anna
& Nora, 13" wide. Estimated
value: $450.

Plate 327. Large Flower Vendor –
Olga with Tina, 11" wide. Estimated value: $550.

Plate 328. Fritz 10". Estimated value: $85. Anna with Tina 9". Scarce. Estimated value: $250.

Plate 329. Olga the Flower Vendor Plaque, 11" wide, 9" tall. Estimated value: $400.

Plates 330. Olga the Flower Vendor with Tina and Basket, 11" wide. Estimated value: $450.

Plate 331. Tina with Basket, 6 ½″ wide. Estimated value: $250.

Plate 333

Plate 332. Anna with Tina 9″. Scarce. Estimated value: $350.

Plate 334

Plates 333 & 334. 11″ Chris and Little Tina. Scarce. Estimated value: $350.

Plate 335. Lisa 10 ½". Estimated value: $175.

Plate 336. Lisa 10 ½" with Little Tina. Scarce. Estimated value: $350.

Plate 339. Cart 3". Estimated value: $45.

Plate 337. Three Geese, 5" to 6". Very scarce, unmarked and very fragile. Estimated value: $100 each.

Plate 338. Barrel 4". Estimated value: $35.

Plate 340. 4" x 4" Fence. Estimated value: $55.

Plate 341. 12" Pennsylvania Dutch Man "Me" and Woman "Thee." Estimated value: $150 each, $350 pair.

Plate 342. Chris 11 ½" and Anna 11". Estimated value: $150 each, $350 pair.

Plate 343. Inga 7" and Chris 7 ½". Estimated value: $75, $100.

Plate 344. Inga 7". Estimated value: $75.

Plate 345. Chris 10". Scarce. Estimated value: $200. Olga 10".
Estimated value: $100.

Plate 347. Tina 6 ½". Estimated value: $65.

Plate 346. Olga 10". Estimated value: $100.

Plate 348 Tina 6 ½". Estimated value: $65.

Plate 351

Plates 351 & 352. Margot 9 ½".
Estimated value: $150.

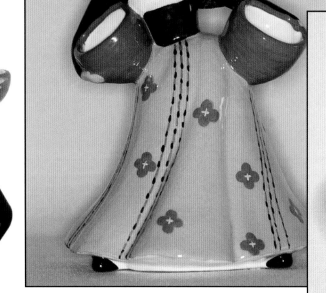

Plate 349. Frieda 11".
Estimated value: $150.

Plate 352

Plate 350. Peg, Liz, Peg 8".
Estimated value: $150 each.

Plate 353. Gretel, Inga, Heidi 5 ½". Estimated value: $50 each.

Plate 354. Gretel 5 ½". Estimated value: $50.

Plate 355. Back view of three peasant children, 5 ½". Each little girl is so unique that they even have different hairdos. Estimated value: $50 each.

Plate 356. Peasant Lady 6".
Estimated value: $55.

Plate 358. Peasant Ladies 5". Estimated value: $50 each.

Plate 357. Peasant Lady 8". Estimated value: $65.

Plate 359. Peasant Lady 8". Estimated value: $65. Peasant man 9". Rare. Estimated value: $250.

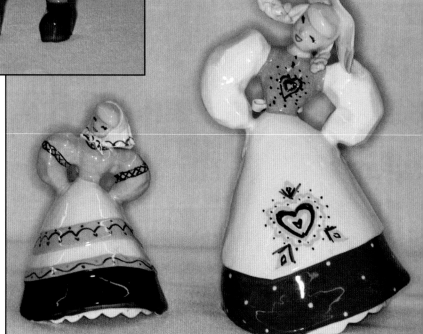

Plate 360. Peasant Lady 5". Estimated value: $50. Peasant Lady 8". Estimated value: $65.

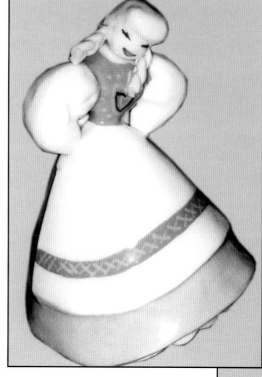

Plate 362. Peasant Lady 6".
Estimated value: $55 each.

Top left & center left:
Plate 361. Peasant Lady 6".
Estimated value: $55 each.

Plate 363. Peasant Ladies 5". Hats vary in style. Estimated value: $50 each.

Plate 364. Jane 3 ½". Estimated value: $50.
Dick 3 ½". Estimated value: $75. Sue 3 ½".
Estimated value: $50.

Plate 365. Jenny 5 ½", Polly 5".
Estimated value: $50 each.

Plate 366. Jenny 5", Sally 5".
Estimated value: $50 each.

Plate 367. Girl 5 ½"
and Boy 4" on
plaque. Scarce.
Estimated value:
$200.

Plate 368. Baby Crawlers 4 ½". Also come with blue polka
dots. Estimated value: $50 each.

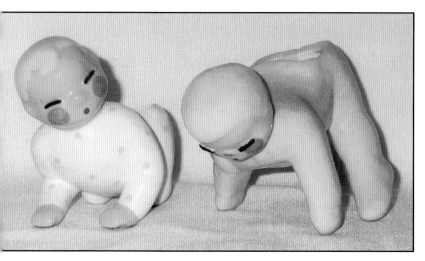

Plate 369. Baby Crawlers. Estimated value: $50, $60.

Plate 370. Baby Pillow Planter 4 ½". Also made with blue and white pillow. Estimated value: $60.

Plate 371. Clyde 9 ½" Horse Flower Container (archival photo). Unmarked and very rare. Estimated value: $550.

The People Bottle Line

Although quite adorable, these pieces were not a big
item for the company and production was quite limited.

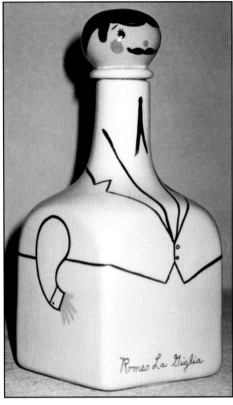

Plate 372

Plates 372 & 373. Romeo La Gilia
9". Estimated value: $500.

Plate 373

Plate 374. Bourbon 10". Estimated
value: $500.

Plate 375. Round Ladies 8".
Estimated value: $400 each.

Plate 376. Round Lady 8".
Estimated value: $400.

Plate 379. Gin Bottle Soldier 10".
Estimated value: $350.

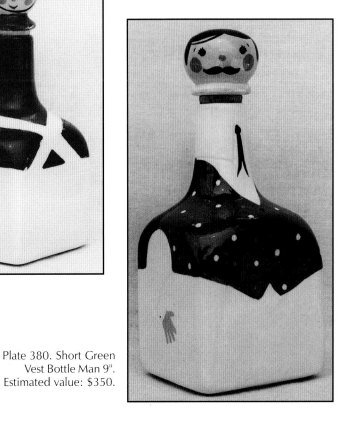

Plate 377. Tall Green Vest
Bottle Man 12". Estimated
value: $500.

Plate 380. Short Green
Vest Bottle Man 9".
Estimated value: $350.

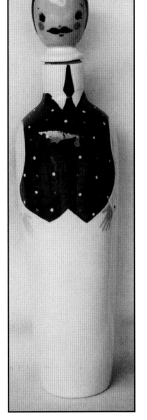

Plate 378. Vodka 8 ½" and
two other Russian Soldier
Bottles 8 ½" each. Estimated
value: $350 each.

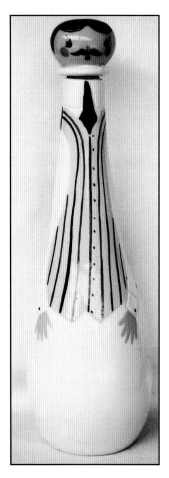

Plate 381. Tall Yellow Vest Man 14 ½". Estimated value: $500.

Plate 385. Big Man 17" and Little Man 8 ½". Estimated value: $500, $350.

Plate 383. Scotch 8 ½". Estimated value: $500.

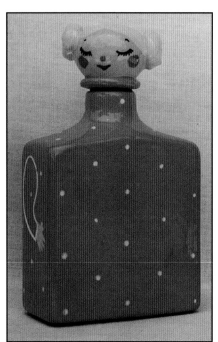

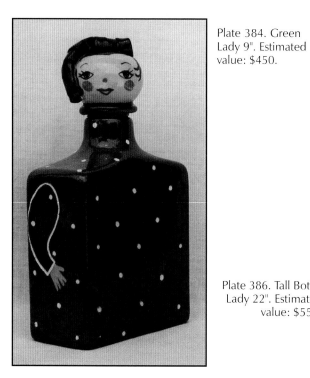

Plate 384. Green Lady 9". Estimated value: $450.

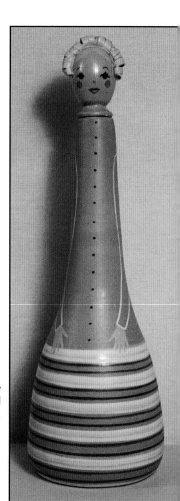

Plate 382. Gold Bottle Lady 9". Estimated value: $450.

Plate 386. Tall Bottle Lady 22". Estimated value: $550.

Plate 387. Tall Bottle Lady 14". Estimated value: $500.

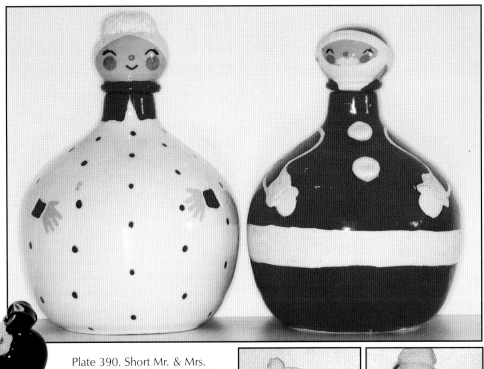

Plate 390. Short Mr. & Mrs. Santa, 8 ½" each. Estimated value: $350 each.

Plate 391. Tall Mr. & Mrs. Santa, 13" each. Estimated value: $550 each.

Plate 388

Plate 389

Plates 388 & 389. Crème de Menthe 8 ½". Estimated value: $600.

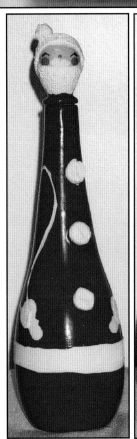

Below: Plate 392. Side view of some of the Bottle People

Betty Lou's Adorable Animal World

As with the early Gay '90s pieces, the artists were given free reign with the early ducks and bunnies, giving them wide divergence in their appearance. As production costs increased and Betty Lou Nichols Ceramics had to be more cost efficient, Betty Lou established a standard pattern for her employees to follow.

The Bunny-Dorables

Plate 394. Flossie 8". Estimated value: $150.

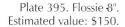

Plate 393. Pierre 9". Estimated value: $175.

Plate 395. Flossie 8". Estimated value: $150.

Plate 396. Flossie 8". Estimated value: $150.

Plate 397. Flossie 8". Personalized for Betty Lou's friends Shirley and Harold. Red nail polish was used on the heart. Estimated value: $200.

Plate 398. Flora 8".
Estimated value: $100.

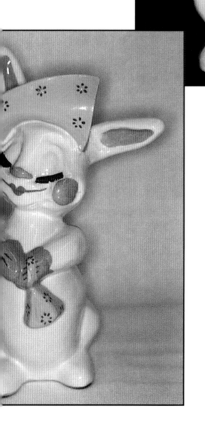

Plate 399. Flossie 8",
8". Estimated value:
$125 each.

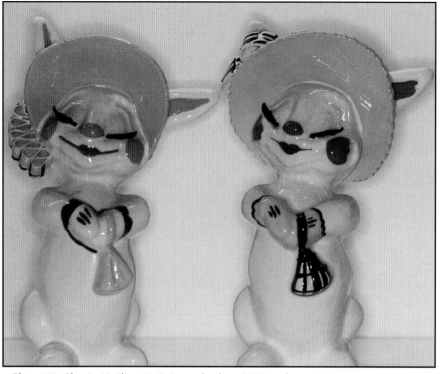

Plate 400. Flossie 8", Flora 8". Estimated value: $100 each.

Plate 401. Charlie 8". Estimated value: $100.

Plate 402. Charlie 8". Estimated value: $100.

Plate 403. Flossie 8", Pierre 9". Estimated value: $375 pair.

Plate 404. Flossie 8", Charlie 8". Estimated value: $250 pair.

Plate 405. Flossie 8", Charlie 8".
Estimated value: $250 pair.

Plate 406. Millie 5", Willie 5".
Estimated value: $100 each.

Plate 407. Millie 5", Willie 5". Estimated value: $100 each.

Plate 408. Millie 5". Estimated value: $100.

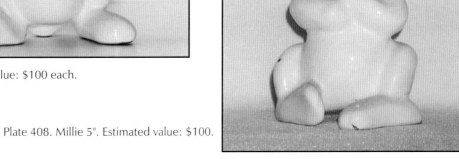

Plate 409. Pete 7 ½", Pamela 6".
Scarce. Estimated value: $150 each.

Plate 410. Boy Bunny 5", Girl
Bunny 5". Estimated value: $100
each.

Plate 411. Nichols' Flora 8". Estimated
value: $100. Japanese copy 7 ½". Estimated
value: $35.

The Ducky-Dorables, Portia Pig, The Birds

Plate 412. Danny 7 ½ ". Estimated value: $100. Dolly 8". Estimated value: $125.

Plate 413. Dolly 8", 8". Estimated value: $125 each.

Plate 414. Danny 7 ½". Estimated value: $100. Dolly 8". Estimated value: $125.

Plate 415. Dolly 8". Estimated value: $125. Danny 7 ½". Estimated value: $100.

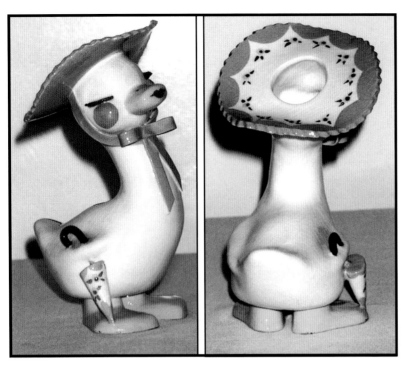

Plate 416. Dolly 8". Estimated value: $125.

Plate 417. Dolly 8". Estimated value: $145.

Plate 418

Plates 418 & 419. Baby Boy Duck 4", Baby Girl Duck 4". Estimated value: $50 each.

Plate 419

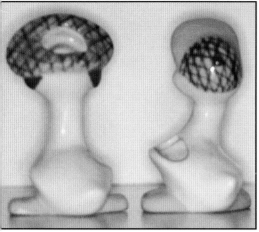

Plate 420

Plates 420 & 421. Back views of Baby Ducks.

Plate 421

Plate 422. Portia Piggy Bank 8", slot in front of bow. Estimated value: $150.

Plate 424

Plates 423 to 425. Portia Pig Planter 8". Estimated value: $150. Japanese copy 7 ¾". Estimated value: $35.

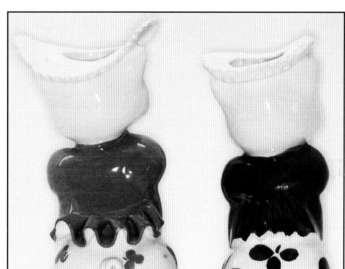

Plate 425

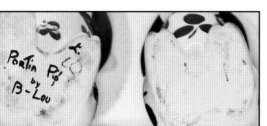

Plate 423

Plate 426

Plates 426 & 427. Song Birds 3". Also come in blue with yellow tips. Estimated value: $50 each.

Plate 427

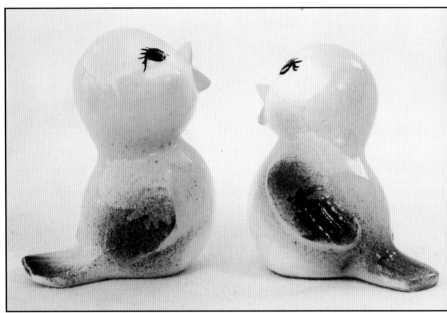

Plate 428. Bird Ashtrays, 7 ½" long, 5" wide. Scarce. Estimated value: $50 each.

The Christmas Line

The Christmas line was very popular. Production would begin in the summer and sell out by the Christmas holiday. Since the red and gold colors required different firing temperatures, many pieces had as many as three separate firings. Normal firing was done in an 1800° kiln. The gold would then be added, requiring a second firing at 900°. Finally the red would be added and the piece baked in an oven at 500°. The artists would often take the Christmas pieces home to paint the red on and then bake them in their home ovens. They were paid 25 cents apiece. You will note inconsistencies in the red color from piece to piece. It was difficult to get a good, bright red Christmas stain, as red does not fire as well as the other colors. This was a problem for all the potters of that time – a problem that is still not completely solved today.

Mr. & Mrs. Santa Claus

Plate 429. Mr. & Mrs. Santa Claus 9", 9 ½". Very old style, Santa has hand-textured hair and beard. Also, Mrs. Santa's eyeglasses were not solid and therefore very fragile. Estimated value: $100 each.

Plate 432

Plate 430. Mr. & Mrs. Santa Revisited 9", 9 ½". Beard and hair texture now added to the mold. Glasses still not solid. Estimated value: Mrs. Santa $100, Mr. Santa $75.

Plates 432 & 433. This 2" x 1 ½" folded insert went into the box containing Mrs. Claus (Mrs. Claus was on the cover of the insert).

Plate 431. Two newer Mrs. Santas 9 ½". Note that the frames of the glasses are filled in. Note also big difference in red coloring. Estimated value: $75 each.

Plate 433

Merry Christmas!

Do you believe in Santa Claus? Of course you do! But didn't your mother ever tell you that there was a **Mrs.** Santa Claus? No? . . . Then, who stays home and takes care of the baby reindeer? Who fills those last minute special orders? Who does the gift wrapping? Who sees that Mr. Claus wears his rubbers and his longies? And who has his pipe and slippers waiting for him when he comes home after his long Christmas ride around the world? . . . . Why, **Mrs.** Santa Claus, of course!

When Johanna Ceramics of Costa Mesa, California decided to close their business, Betty Lou Nichols purchased some of their molds. [Their pieces will be marked with an asterisk (*).] However, there were always modifications and improvements made by Nichols Ceramics.

Plate 434*. Large Santas 9 ½". Note cheek color in distinct circles typical of Nichols pieces. Estimated value: $100 each.

Plate 435*. Johanna Santa 9 ½". Note how red color is just splashed across the face. Estimated value: $40.

Plate 436*. Medium Santa 6 ½". Also comes in white. Estimated value: $65.

Plate 437*. Johanna large and medium Santas with cheek color similar to Plate 435.

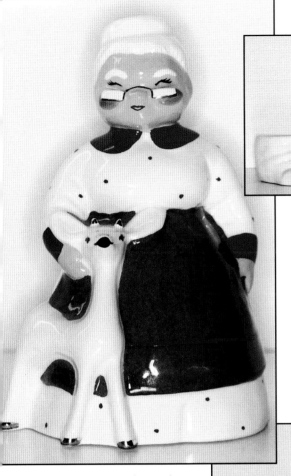

Plate 439. Santa with Bag, Santa with Box, Reclining Santa with Bag, 4" to 5". All also come with Santas in red. Estimated value: $45 each.

Plate 438. Mrs. Santa with Reindeer 6 ½". Estimated value: $75.

Plate 440. Santa with Sled, 5 ½" x 8", Santa with Bag 7". Both also come with white Santas. Estimated value: $50 each.

Plate 441*. Santa Bank 3". Johanna Santa on left, Nichols' Santa on right. Estimated value: $30, $60.

119

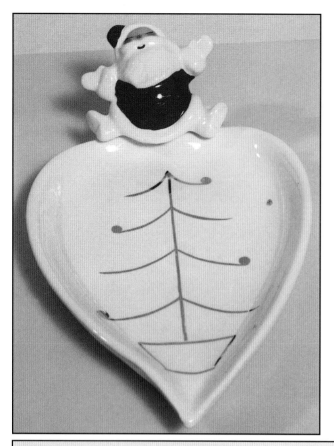

Top left: Plate 442. Santa Candy Dish, 10 x 6 ½". Comes with six poses of little Santas. Estimated value: $70.

Top right: Plate 443. Santa Candy Dish. Note Santa's different pose. Estimated value: $70.

Plate 444. Santa Cookie Jar 5 ¼". Estimated value: $80.

Plate 445

Plate 446

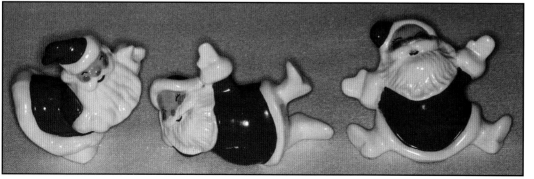

Plates 445 & 446*. Little Santas came in six poses, 2" each. These were the original batch of small Santas made from the Johanna molds. Betty Lou felt these were not cute enough and the heads were too small so she remade them with larger heads and different faces, poses, and hats. Estimated value: $20 each.

Plate 448

Plate 447

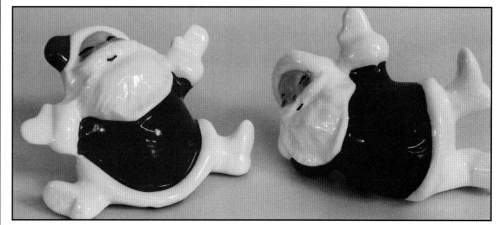

Plate 449

Plates 447 to 449. New improved version of Little Santas. Estimated value: $50 each.

Plate 450

Plate 451

Plates 450 & 451. These photos show the old style Santas on the left and new versions on the right.

Plate 452

Plate 454. Mr. Grab Bag 9". Jack is a separate piece. Comes in black or red. Estimated value: with Jack $150, without Jack $75. Also comes in 6". Estimated value: $65.

POST CARD

READY REINDEER

Mr. S. Claus's reindeer vacation incognito at Palm Springs to get ready for their annual job. Mr. and Mrs. Claus and the Merry Hustlers, Dick, Tom and Holly are already hard at work.

Use them in eye-catching displays and in your advertising to build store traffic and play a merry sales tune on your cash register.

Reindeer are approximately 12" high, the sleigh 14". Two of the Merry Hustlers, Dick and Tom are 5½" and Holly is 6½" high. Mr. and Mrs. Claus are 9" high. All are individually packed and F.O.B. La Habra, California. Terms: 2/10 E.O.M.

Prices (wholesale):

Mr. and Mrs. Claus	$6.50 per pair
Reindeer	3.00 each
Sleigh	2.50 each
Dick and Tom	2.25 each
Holly	2.00 each

ORDER FROM

Ruth Sloan

1003 Brack Shop   1500 Merchandise Mart
527 West 7th Street   Chicago 54,
Los Angeles 14, Calif.   Illinois
Form 3547 Requested

STAMP

ANGELENO PHOTO SERVICE • LOS

Plate 453

Plates 452 & 453. Front and back of Ruth Sloan's order form post card.

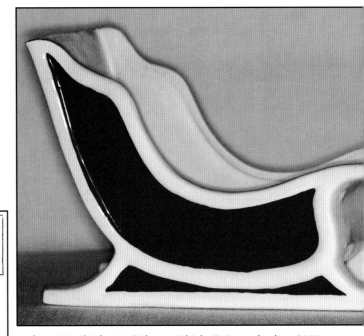

Plate 455. Sleigh, 11 ½" long, 8" high. Estimated value: $100.

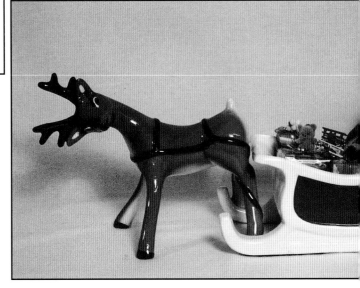

Plate 456. Sleigh 7 ½" with "Ready" Reindeer. Estimated value: $225 pair.

Plate 457. Sleigh 6 ½" with small reindeer 6".
Estimated value: $375 for set.

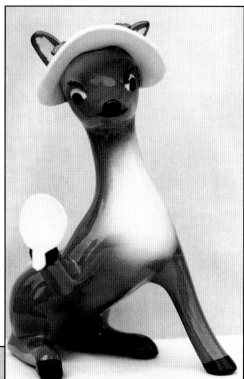

Plate 458. Duchess 8". First of the "Ready
Reindeer," also known as the "Palm Springs
Reindeer." Estimated value: $125.

Plate 459. Duke 8". Estimated
value: $125.

Plate 460. Waldo, 6 ½" high
9 ½" long. Estimated value:
$125.

Plate 462. Herbert, 11" long.
Estimated value: $125.

Plate 461. Freddy, 9" high.
Estimated value: $125.

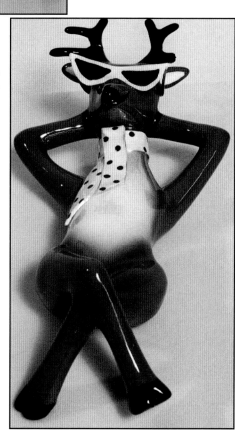

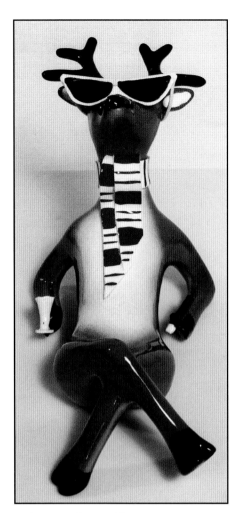

Plate 463. Sam, 11" long.
Estimated value: $125.

Plate 464. Donnie, 4" high.
Estimated value: $100.

Plate 465. Reindeer Trio.

Plate 466. Mr. Snowman 8 ½", Mrs. Snowman 7 ½".
Estimated value: $60 each, $150 pair.

Plate 467. Miniature Mr. And Mrs. Snowman 3", sometimes with
holes for salt and pepper. Estimated value: $40 each, $100 pair.

Plate 468

Plate 469

Plates 468 to 470. Punch Bowl, 5" high ,diameter 12". Santa's whip wraps around the bowl spelling out Merry Christmas. Mugs are all alike. Estimated value: Punch Bowl $400, Ladle $200, Santa Mugs $50 each.

Plate 470

Plate 471

Plate 472

Plates 471 & 472. Christmas Tree Cookie Jars 9", 6". Estimated value: $150, $75.

125

Plate 473

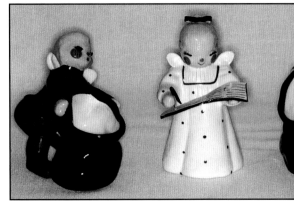

Plates 473 & 474. Tom, Dick & Holly. Tom and Dick also come with green bags. Estimated value: $50 each, $200 set.

Plate 474

Plate 478

Plate 475

Plate 479

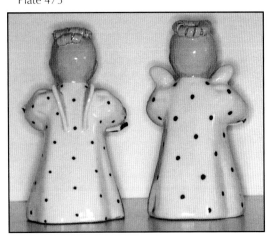

Plate 476

Plates 475 & 476. Two Hollys. Note differences in hairstyles and wings. Estimated value: $50 each.

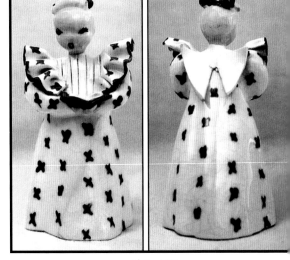

Plate 480

Plate 477. Praying Angel 6 ½", Singing Angel 8", Kneeling Angel 5 ½". Crowns hold 1" diameter candle, cheeks may vary in color. Estimated value: $55 each.

Plates 478 to 480. Girls Choir (Angels) 4 ½". These were all very early Betty Lou pieces. Hair curls are all styled differently, as are the colors. The décor appears to be random. Some hold books; some were designed to hold candles. The wings were often broken off of these fragile pieces. Scarce. Estimated value: $125 each.

Plate 481. Choir Boys 4". Very scarce. Estimated value: $200 each.

Plate 482

Plate 482 to 484. Black choir figures. Boys 4", girls 4 ¼". Extremely rare. Estimated value: $300 each.

Plate 483

Plate 484

Plate 486. Small and large mugs. Estimated value: small $35 each, large $40 each.

Plate 487. Matched plate and mug sets. Estimated value: $150 each.

Plate 488. Luanne's mug. Estimated value: $50.

Opposite page: Plate 485. Just a small sample of Betty Lou's plates are included here. Luanne Nichols Shoup said that there was no need to wallpaper her kitchen when she could decorate it with her mother's unending line of plates. Estimated value: Gay '90s plates $200 each; peasant girl and boy plates $150 each; fruit, flower and bird plates $100 each; ribbon plates $125 each.

Unique Items

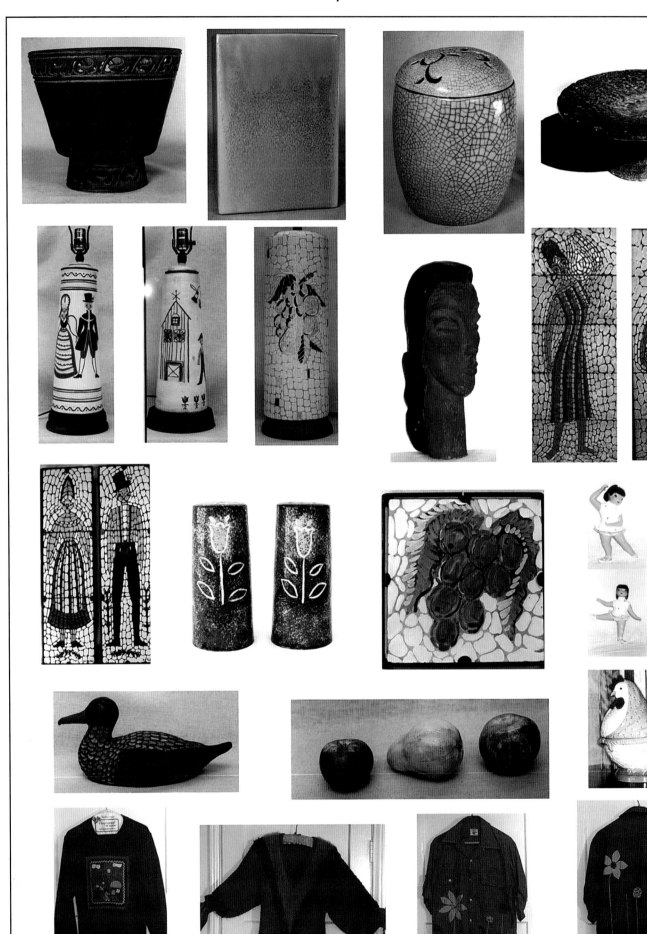

Miscellaneous Items

Fantasia Babies and Hippos

Plate 490

Plate 493

Plate 492

Plates 490 to 493. The 3" Fantasia Babies were fashioned after the babies in the animated movie *Fantasia* and sold at Disneyland (Anaheim, California) in the gift shops. They were not a big seller and consequently were in production for only a short period (1959 and 1960). Notice that the flesh is a flat glaze, which was very unlike Betty Lou's style. Also, there were problems getting the wings to adhere to the body. These pieces are unmarked and very rare. Since they were too small to have any markings, a tiny Walt Disney stamp (only ½" in diameter) was affixed to the wings. Estimated value: $40 each.

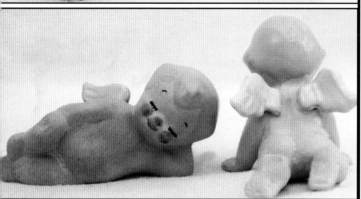

Plate 491

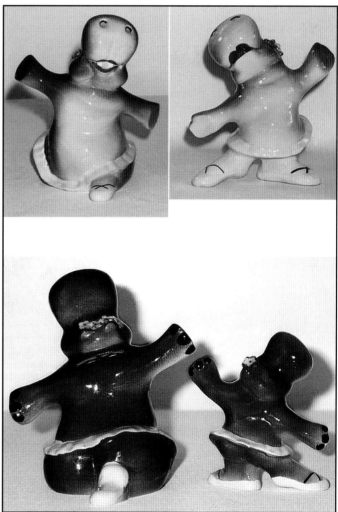

Plate 494. Hippos from the animated movie *Fantasia*. The large hippo has a slot in the back to put money in. Like the Fantasia babies, these were designed for Walt Disney Productions to be sold at the Disneyland gift stores. Estimated value: 5 ½", $50; 4 ½", $40.

Opposite page: Plate 489. Unique items owned by Betty Lou's family members. It is impossible to estimate their value.

Eggs and Tea Sets

Plate 495. Easter Eggs, 3" x 3 ½" a 4 ½" x 7 ½", ma for the florists. Came in several colors. Estimated value: $40, $70.

Plates 496 & 497. Tea Set 3 ½", 6", 3 ½". Estimated value per set: $300.

Plate 496

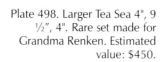

Plate 497

Plate 498. Larger Tea Sea 4", 9 ½", 4". Rare set made for Grandma Renken. Estimated value: $450.

The Nodders

A touch of the hand makes these heads nod yes and no. The easiest to find are Percy and Prissy, followed by the Cat and Mouse and the Rabbits. The Elephant and Donkey are the scarcest.

Plate 499. Percy Nodder and Prissie Nodder. Estimated value: $200 pair.

Plate 500. Funny Nodder and Honey Nodder. Estimated value: $250 pair.

Plate 501. Tom Cat Nodder and Twerpie Nodder. Estimated value: $250 pair.

Plate 502. Elephant Nodder and Donkey Nodder. Estimated value: $300 pair.

Boxes

Plate 503. Box, 3" x 6". Estimated value: $300 each.

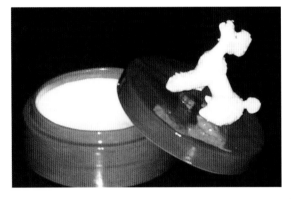

Plate 504. Poodle Powder Box customized for Betty Lou's friend Shirley. Estimated value: $350.

Plate 506. Powder Box, 5 ½" x 5 ½". One of a kind made for Grandma Renken. Estimated value: $350.

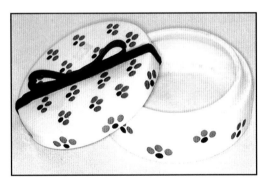

Plate 507. Boxes, 9" diameter, 6" diameter. Estimated value: $300, $200.

Plate 505. Powder Boxes, 3 ½" x 5 ½". Estimated value: $300 each.

Plate 508. Florabelle Hat Box, 2" x 6" x 7". These also come with a lid. Estimated value: $400.

Jam Jars and Syrup Pitchers

Plate 509. Jam Jar 5" and Syrup Pitcher 4" made for Knott's Berry Farm. Lots and lots of these were made. This was the last production of Betty Lou Nichols Ceramics. After Betty Lou stopped producing them they were made in Japan. Estimated value: $150 pair.

Plate 510. Betty Lou jar (left) and Japanese copy. Note the very subtle differences. Betty Lou's berries are purple; the Japanese berries are blue.

Plate 511. Betty Lou Nichols stamp reads "Hand Painted" in the middle.

Plate 512. Another Japanese jar and pitcher. Although these read "hand painted" on the bottom, they are easy to tell apart from the original. They differ in size (4" each) and the berries are three dimensional instead of flat.

135

The Paintings

Plate 513

Plate 514

Plate 515

Plates 513 to 521. When Betty Lou Nichols closed her ceramics company in 1962 – on her fortieth birthday – she rechanneled her artistic energies into painting. While she was already known nationally for her work in ceramics, she soon gained recognition for her character studies and landscapes as she turned to painting full time. In fact, she became better known as painter than as a ceramist especially in California and Arizona. Betty Lou spent over half her productive life as a painter and is only now beginning to gain national recognition in that area. Since very few of her paintings have been offered for sale, it is very difficult to accurately estimate their value.

Plate 516

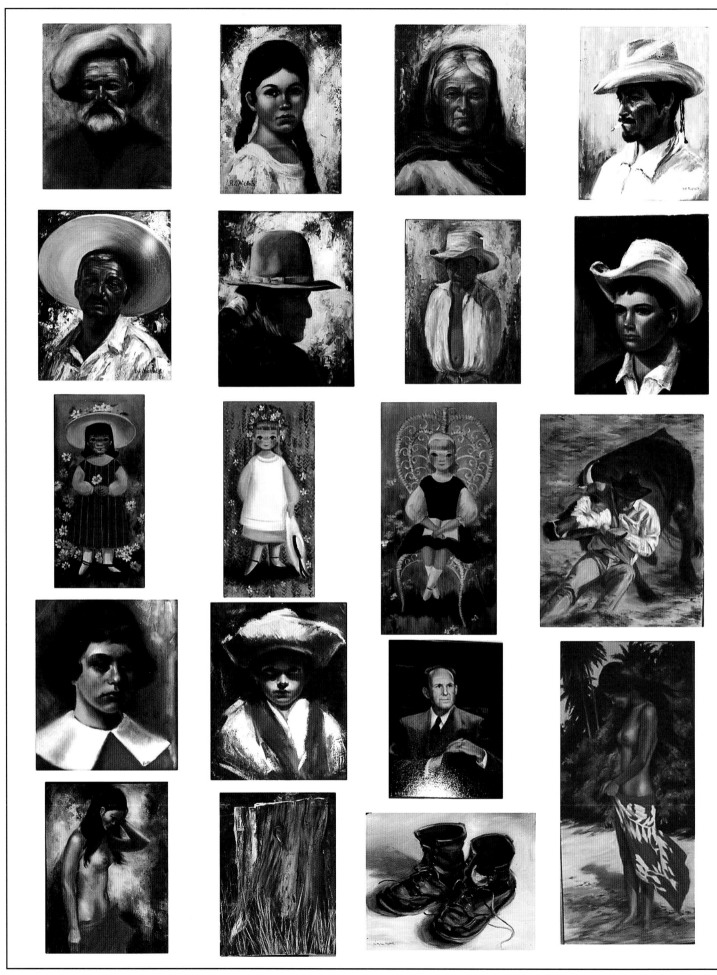

Plate 517

Plate 518

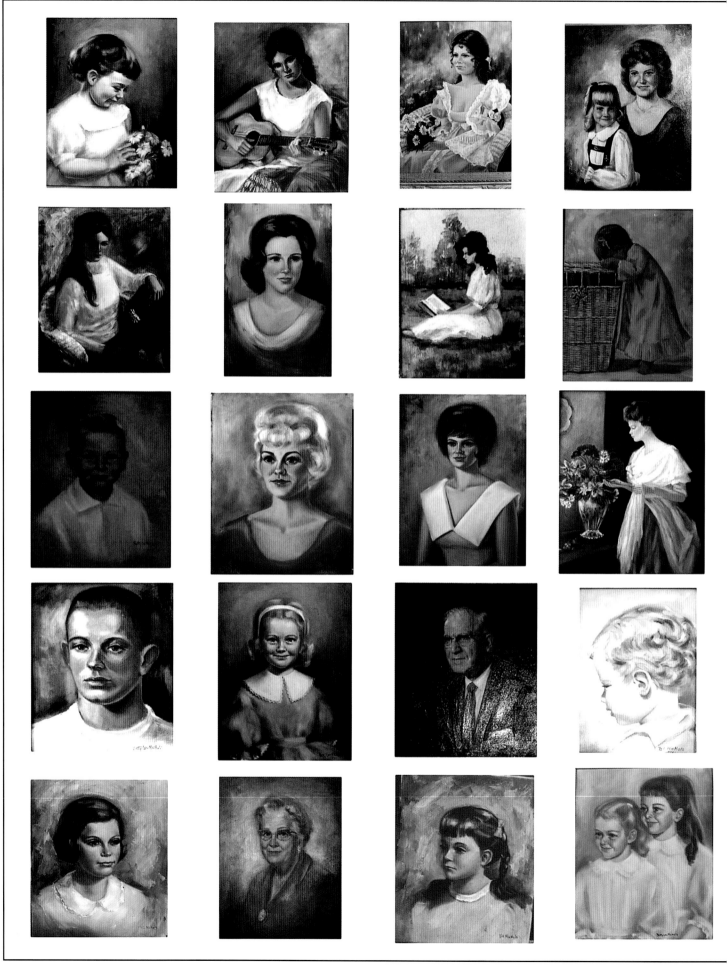

Plate 519

Plate 520

Plate 521

Ruth Sloan

Jan 1951

1003 Brack Shop Bldg., 527 West Seventh St., Los Angeles 14, Calif.
TUcker 6231

Bunny-dorables 8"
Flora, Flopsie & Flossie   33.00 dz
Charlie M'Boy & Pierre   36.00 dz

FLORA-DORABLES

By Betty Lou Nichols

F.O.B. LaHabra, Calif.
Terms 2%   10 net 30
Prices wholesale

Registered CALIFORNIA

Portia Pig
7½"   36.00 dz

Luanne
10½"   6.25 ea

Florabelle
11" 8.75 ea

Ermintrude
8"   6.25
6"   3.75

Nellie
8"   6.25
6"   3.75

Linda Lou
8"   6.25
6"   3.75

Mary Lou
8"   6.25
6"   3.75

Nancy Lou
8"   6.25
6"   3.75

Valerie
8"   6.25
6"   3.75

YOUNG - ADORABLES   36.00 dz.

Polly   Jill   Becky   Tom   Kathy   Judy

The catalogs on this and the following pages are from
Betty Lou Nichols' sales representatives – Ruth Sloan and W.A. Curie, Inc.

2 Lili 7" **$45.00** dz.   H-15 Vicki **$30.00** dz.   H-12 Suzanne 7" **$48.00** dz.
H-1 Lili 9" **$75.00** dz.   H-11 Suzanne 9" **$78.00** dz.

300 Virginia 10" **$17.50** each   301 Georgia 10" **$17.50** each
304 Melanie 8"   306 Melanie Ann 5"   305 Emmy Lou 5"   303 Emmy 8"
$30.00 dz.   **$18.00** dz.   **$18.00** dz.   **$30.00** dz.

BETTY LOU NICHOLS

Ceramics

"Nothing could be finer in
CALIFORNIA CERAMICS"

WHOLESALE
PRICE
LIST

★ FEATURING
BETTY LOU'S original
Flora-Dorables and figurines

-4 Mitzi 7"   H-13 Girl Demi   H-14 Boy Demi   H-6 Ann 7"
$45.00 dz.   **$12.00** dz.   **$12.00** dz.   **$45.00** dz.
H-3 Mitzi 9" **$75.00** dz.   H-5 Ann 9" **$75.00** dz.

Terms: 2%, 10 days; F.O.B. La Habra, Calif.

DISTRIBUTED BY

W. A. CURRIE, INC.

527 WEST SEVENTH ST.
LOS ANGELES 14
CALIFORNIA

144

Ruth Sloan

1003 Brack Shop Bldg., 527 West Seventh St., Los Angeles 14, Calif.
TUcker 6231

1500 Merchandise Mart, Chicago 54, Illinois
WHitehall 4-3126

FLORA-DORABLES
BY BETTY LOU NICHOLS

LOUISA

CYNTHIA

6 Styles - 6" or 8" Sizes
6" - 3.75 ea
8" - 6.25 ea

CANDY

SHEILA

VICKY

MICHELLE

LUANNE
10½" 6.25 ea

FLORABELLE
11" 8.75 ea

THE DEMI-DORABLES
MARCY, MAGGIE, MIMI - 3" high, 12.00 dz

Ceramic Hat Boxes for Cigarettes, Sweetmeats, Powder Puffs -- 24.00 dz
Hat Box Ashtrays, assorted color trims to match boxes   -- 12.00 dz

F.O.B: La Habra   Prices Wholesale   No Packing Charge   Terms: 2/10 EOM
Low Cost Freight Shipments at 20.00 Released Valuation Fully Insured Thru CAPA

145

FLORISTS' FOTOQUIZ
by Ruth Sloan

Below are some of the many new items designed especially for florists by BETTY LOU NICHOLS.
Study each photo and caption carefully, and your "sales score" will be highly profitable.

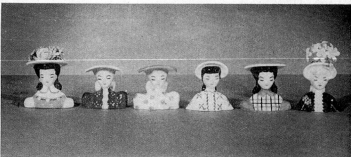

HOW MUCH ARE EGG HEADS?
Only $12.00 per dozen for small (5") size and $4.00 each for large (9") size. Order now for Easter delivery!

ARE DEMI-DORABLES STILL ONLY $12.00 PER DOZEN?
Correct! Prove this by ordering today from your nearest representative.

ARE DUCKY-DORABLES EXPENSIVE?
No! These proven best-sellers are $12.00 per dozen in the small (4") size, and the large sizes (8") are offered at $30.00 a dozen.

HOW MUCH DO THE FLOWER CONTAINER MADONNAS COST?
Betty Lou Nichols beautiful Madonnas come in three sizes: Miniatures (4") $12.00 dozen.—Medium size (7½") $3.75 each. Large size (9") $7.50 each.

CAN I ORDER A SAMPLE ASSORTMENT?

6 Small Egg Heads		6.00
3 Small Rabbits		6.00
1 pr. Mr. & Mrs. Rabbit		5.50
6 Small Ducks		6.00
1 pr. Mr. & Mrs. Duck		5.00
6 Demi-Dorables		6.00
4 Miniature Madonnas		4.00
29 Pieces	**YES!**	**38.50**

ARE BUNNY-DORABLES GOOD EASTER SELLERS?
Yes! At $24.00 per dozen for the small (5") size and only $2.50 each for Mrs. and $3.00 for Mr. Rabbit, Betty Lou Nichols Bunny-Dorables are sure-fire Easter hits.

WHAT IS THE "BAKER'S GROSS" DEAL?
For a limited time only, gross orders for the $12.00 per dozen items will come packed with an extra 12 pieces (a bonus dozen per gross). A $312.00 retail value for only $144.00 net.

BETTY LOU NICHOLS

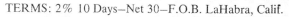

Ceramics

9½" Figurines...$78.00 doz. Left to Right
F-1 Cecile Lemon Yellow: F-2 Virginia Soft Pink
F-3 Stephanie White & Gold; F-4 Belinda White

The Betty Lou Nichols touch...in every piece evidence of the extra care and skill, the conscious pride of true craftsmanshp...there are no "short-cuts" in the making of a Betty Lou piece.

Each item is an original, entirely hand decorated in soft, subtle colors...warm pinks, cool turquoise, rich greens and browns...colors pleasing to the eye and reflect quiet beauty.

9½" Figurines...$78.00 doz. Left to Right
F-5 Angela Sage Green: F-6 Rosalyn White w/Pink
F-7 Melissa Black & White: F-8 Jessica Green & White

7" Figurines...$42.00 doz. Left to Right
F-14 Madelon Black w/White: F-15 Milicent Pink
F-16 Felicie White w/Gold: F-17 Laurie Green
F-18 Becky Turquoise: F-19 Charlotte Brown w/Pink

WHOLESALE PRICE LIST

W. A. CURRIE, Inc.

527 WEST SEVENTH ST., LOS ANGELES, CALIF.
204 BRACK SHOPS—TRinity 7678

148

Ruth Sloan

1003 Brack Shop Bldg., 527 West Seventh St., Los Angeles 14, Calif.
TUcker 6231

1500 Merchandise Mart, Chicago 54, Illinois
WHitehall 4-3126

Betty Lou Nichols' delightful
PLEASANT
PEASANT series

Registered CALIFORNIA

Large Flower Vendor

Gossip Plaque

Olga
Flower Vendor

Olga & Tina

Chris - Tall Man, 11"	3.25 ea
Lisa - Tall Girl, 10½"	3.25 ea
Tina w/Cart or Basket, 5½"	2.50 ea
Tommy w/Cart or Basket, 5½"	2.50 ea
Anna - Fat Mamma, 9"	3.25 ea
Fritz w/Barrel, 9½"	3.50 ea
Nora - Gossip, 9½"	3.25 ea
Clyde - Horse Flower Container, 9½"	8.75 ea
Large Plaque - Olga Flower Vendor w/Tina	16.25 ea
Gossip Plaque - Anna & Nora	14.75 ea
Olga - Flower Vendor	6.25 ea
Olga Flower Vendor w/Tina & Basket	7.50 ea
Fence Flower Container	12.00 dz
Geese	7.20 dz
Barrel	6.00 dz
Basket Pot Containers	4.80 & 6.00 dz

Tina & Tommy

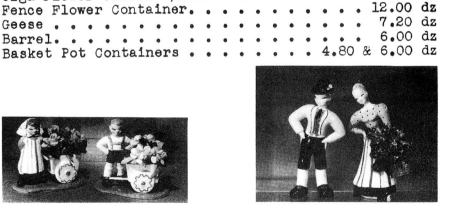

Chris & Lisa

Clyde

Fritz & Anna

F.O.B: La Habra   Prices Wholesale   Terms: 2/10 EOM
3% Packing Charge on Orders under 100.00   No Packing Charge on Orders above 100.00
Low Cost Freight Shipments @ 20.00 Released Valuation Fully Insured thru CAPA

149

Presenting BETTY LOU NICHOLS' charming new Provinçial and Early American family... decorated in fresh, crisp color combinations of lemon, rust, orange, green, brown, black and white...the perfect accent pieces for Provincial decor.

Pennsylvania Dutch decor in Brown—12″
F-25 Man "Me" ....$36.00 doz.
F-26 Woman "Thee" .... 36.00 doz.
F-36 Baskets Large or Medium............. 4.50 doz.

F-27 Anna 11″ Green, White & Black Comb.... $36.00 doz.
F-28 Chris 11½″ Rust, Orange & White Comb.. 36.00 doz.
F-37 Geese $4.50 doz.: F-36 Basket Small..... 4.50 doz.

F-28 Olga 10″ Rust, Black & White Comb..... $36.00 doz.
F-32 Inga 7″ White, Brown & Black Comb..... 24.00 doz.
F-31 Tina 6½″ Green & White Combination... 21.00 doz.
F-30 Hans 7″ Lemon, Green & Black Comb... 21.00 doz.

"Nothing could be finer in CALIFORNIA CERAMICS"

BETTY LOU NICHOLS...
Ceramics

F-49 Large Madonna 10".................$60.00 doz.
F-48 Medium Madonna 8"................ 36.00 doz.
F-50 Angels: Kneeling, Singing, Praying...... 30.00 doz.
       Decorated with 22 Carat Gold Special Fire

F-58 Demi-dorables: Boy & Girl
       Assorted colors ....Pack 12...$12.00 doz.
F-59 Baby Crawler Asst'd. colors...Pack 12... 12.00 doz.
F-57 Eggheads Asst'd. 4 styles.....Pack 12... 12.00 doz.
F-40 Melanie 8" Asst'd color............... 30.00 doz.
F-43 Melanie Ann 5" Asst'd colors.......... 18.00 doz.

F-72 Elephant Nodder..........Pack 12...$12.00 doz.
F-71 Donkey Nodder...........Pack 12... 12.00 doz.

The Nodder Family...a touch of your hand or a slight draft in a room makes these come alive. Their heads nod "Yes" or "No".

This, being Election Year, both Elephant and Donkey are hopeful...both nod "Yes".

F-65 Percy Nodder ....$18.00 doz.
F-66 Prissie Nodder .... 18.00 doz.
F-69 Tom Cat Nodder .... 18.00 doz.
F-70 Twerpie Mouse Nodder.............. 18.00 doz.

PLANTERS: 205 Baby Duck **$12.00** dz.   204 Mrs. Duck   203 Mr. Duck **$30.00** dz.

MADONNAS: 100 **$12.00** dz.   101 **$36.00** dz.   102 **$60.00** dz.
ANGELS: 106 **$18.00** dz.   105 **$30.00** dz.   104 **$30.00** dz.   103 **$30.00** dz.

P-7 **$12.00** dz.
BIRD ASH TRAYS: P-8 **$12.00** dz.   P-6 **$12.00** dz.

PLANTERS: 206-B Bear   206-A Lamb   206-C Elephant **$18.00** dz.
208 Baby Crawler **$12.00** dz.   207 Pig Bank **$18.00** dz.

X-54 Dick   X-55 Holly   X-53 Tom   X-56 Choir Boy
$27.00 dz.   **$24.00** dz.   **$27.00** dz.   **$18.00** dz.
X-22 Santa Bank **$18.00** dz.

H-8 Nanette 7" **$48.00** dz.   H-10 Collette 7" **$48.00** dz.
H-7 Nanette 9" **$78.00** dz.   H-9 Collette 9" **$78.00** dz.

N-22 Funny **$18.00** dz.   N-23 Honey **$18.00** dz.   N-26 Sabrina **$36.00** dz.
N-24 Tom Cat   N-25 Twerpie Mouse   N-21 Prissie   N-20 Percy
$18.00 dz.   **$18.00** dz.   **$18.00** dz.   **$18.00** dz.

"Nothing could be finer in
CALIFORNIA CERAMICS"

BETTY LOU NICHOLS...
Ceramics

P-2 "Thee" 12" **$39.00** dz.   P-1 "Me" 12" **$39.00** dz.

402 Gretel **$24.00** dz.   401 Inga **$24.00** dz.   400 Heidi **$24.00** dz.   202 Small Egg Heads **$12.00** dz. asst.

THE EASTER PARADE!

Sassy Bunnies and Ducks all dressed up in their Easter bonnets with all the frills upon it...cleverly designed floral containers...a fresh flower completes their ensemble. Soft pastel Easter colors used on all items.

Their heads, perfectly balanced, nod "Yes" or "No" at the slightest touch. You'll love their whimsical appeal.

F-51 Large Boy & Girl Rabbit...........$21.00 doz. pcs.
F-52 Small Boy & Girl Rabbit........... 7.50 doz. pcs.
Above numbers come in assorted colors of
Yellow, Pink, Turquoise & Purple

F-53 Large Boy & Girl Duck...........$30.00 doz. pcs.
F-54 Small Boy & Girl Duck........... 7.50 doz. pcs.
Above numbers come in assorted pastel colors
on white bodies

X-8 Santa, Red or White, 6½″ High........$24.00 dz
X-10 Mrs. Claus—Med., 6½″ High......... 24.00 dz
X-19 Mr. Santa Claus—Lg., 9½″ High...... 36.00 dz
X-20 Mrs. Santa Claus—Lg., 9½″ High...... 36.00 dz

X-13 Mr. Snowman, 8½″ High...........$18.00 dz
X-14 Mrs. Snowman, 7½″ High........... 18.00 dz
X-17 Snowman Salt & Pepper, Min. 1 dz.... 12.00 dz pr

Top Row—Left to Right
X-9 Santa w/Bag—sitting, Red or White......$24.00 dz
X-6 Santa w/Box—Red or White........... 24.00 dz
X-7 Santa w/Bag—standing, Red or White.... 24.00 dz
Bottom Row—Left to Right
X-4 Santa w/Sled—Red or White........... 24.00 dz
X-8 Santa—standing, Red or White......... 24.00 dz
X-5 Santa w/Bag—lying, Red or White....... 24.00 dz

X-11 Santa Candy Box, 8x5x2½″, Assorted
    Decor., Minimum 6 assorted..........$24.00 dz
X-12 Santa Candy Dish, 10x6½″, Assorted
    Decor., Minimum 6 assorted.......... 18.00 dz
X-18 Miniature Santas—6 styles Assorted
    Minimum 1 dz..................... 7.20 dz

Betty Lou Nichols Christmas Family

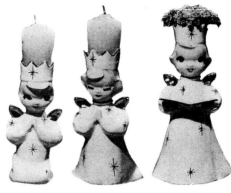

MR. & MRS. S. CLAUS (9") - 13.00 pair
THE MERRY HUSTLERS (5½")   Dick - Tom - 4.50 each
Holly - 4.00 each

Kneeling Angel (6½") - 5.00 each
Praying Angel (6½") - 5.00 each
Singing Angel (8") - 5.00 each

Duchess (8") - 6.00 each   Duke (8") - 6.00 each
Donnie (4") - 4.00 each   Blitz (4") - 4.00 each   Freddy

READY REINDEER (9") - 6.00 each
George
Sam
Elmo
Herbie

Red & White Sleigh, 14" - 6.00 each
Waldo 3.00 each   FREDDY

156

happy holiday hits

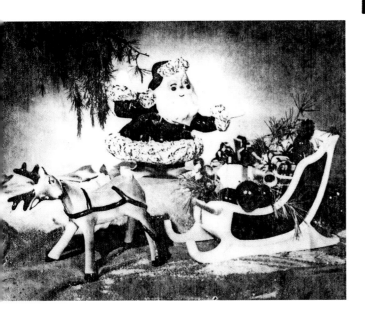

The finest, most appealing, best priced Christmas decoration line available. To display them is to sell them. Bright reds and greens or crisp clean white, all highlighted with gleaming gold trim expertly applied. You will find this line the most profitable you have ever sold. Place your order early for guaranteed delivery.

W. A. CURRIE, Inc.

527 WEST SEVENTH ST., LOS ANGELES, CALIF.
204 BRACK SHOPS—TRinity 7678

WHOLESALE PRICE LIST

TERMS: 2% 10 Days—Net 30—F.O.B. LaHabra, Calif.

X-23 Santa Claus, 9½", Red or White....... $78.00 dz
X-21 Reindeer, 7½" High .... 36.00 dz
X-22 Large Sleigh, 12" Long................ 36.00 dz

X-8 Santa Standing, 6½" High, Red or White . $24.00 dz
X-16 Reindeer, 6" High, Min. 1 dz.......... 15.00 dz
X-15 Sleigh, 6½" Long, Red or White........ 18.00 dz

X-1 Punch Bowl .... $42.00 dz
X-2 Ladle .... 12.00 dz
X-3 Santa Mugs .... 9.00 dz

X-24 Santa 6½"
$24.00 dz.

X-29 Santa w/chimney
$24.00 dz.

X-14 Santa w/sled $24.00 dz.

X-8 Santa Candleholder
$24.00 dz.

X-3 Santa Claus 10" $78.00 dz.

X-6 Sleigh 5"x8" $30.00 dz.

X-27 Reindeer 6" $30.00 dz.

HAPPY HOLIDAY hits .....

X-52 Sleigh 14" $36.00 dz.

X-41 Mrs. S. Claus $39.00 dz.

X-40 Mr. S. Claus $39.00 dz.

X-19 Reindeer $7.20 dz.

X-16 Min. Santa Claus $7.20 dz. asst.

X-42 Sam 9" $36.00 dz.
X-45 Herbie 9"
$36.00 dz.

X-50 Donnie 4" $24.00 dz.
X-44 Elmo 9"
$36.00 dz.

X-51 Blitz 4"
$24.00 dz.

X-49 Waldo 9" $36.00 dz.
X-43 George 9"
$36.00 dz.

X-2 Punch Bowl $42.00 dz.

X-26 Santa Mug $9.00 dz.

X-28 Ladle $12.00 dz.

X-21 Santa Candy Jar $30.00 dz.

The Marks

At the very beginning of production (the Gay '90s Figurines), Betty Lou would sign her name "B'Lou" painted by hand underglaze. As the business grew, she changed this to "Betty Lou Nichols" and she had whichever artist painted the ceramics sign for her as well as initial the piece, also underglaze. This was usually done in block letters but occasionally the artist would sign in script. All the head vases were sent out of the factory with scalloped felt on the bottoms to protect the surfaces that the heads would rest on.

Later pieces had inked stamped marks that read "Betty Lou Nichols Copyright," "Betty Lou Nichols La Habra, California" or other variations. Occasionally, paper labels were used. Sometimes a registered California paper label was added. A few pieces read "Copyright Ruth Sloan."

Many pieces are unmarked. Sometimes this was caused by human error, sometimes the piece was too small to sign. Often the inked stamped marks have faded or have been rubbed off. Look carefully – sometimes the faded traces of a mark can still be seen.

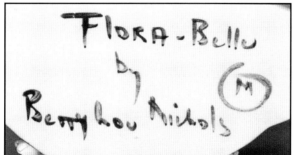

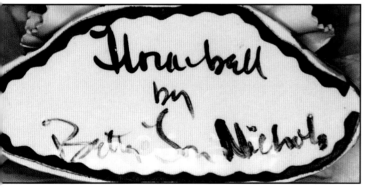

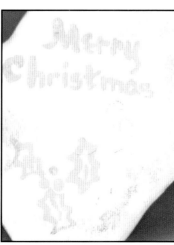

Bibliography

Head Vases

Barron, Dave and Yvonne. *Head Vases by number Price Guide* PO Box 7901 Columbus, MS 37705 (e-mail: dlb@ebicom.net) updated annually.

Cole, Kathleen. *Head Vases.* Paducah, KY: Collector Books, 1989.

Cole, Kathleen. *Encyclopedia of Head Vases.* Atglen, PA: Schiffer Publishing Ltd., 1996.

Gipson, Polly. *Face to Vase with Glamour Gals.* Weston, Oregon: 1988

Gordon, Maddy. *Head Hunters Newsletter* PO Box 83H Scarsdale, NY 10583, published quarterly 914-472-0200 e-mail: maddy.gordon@worldnet.att.net

Gordon, Maddy. Annual *Head Hunters Convention* PO Box 83H, Scarsdale, NY 10583

Posgay, Mike and Ian Warner. *The World of Head Vase Planters.* Marietta, Ohio: Antique Publications 1992.

Zavada, Mary. *Lady Head Vases.* Atglen, Pennsylvania: Schiffer Publishing Ltd., 1988.

California Pottery

Chipman, Jack. *Collectors Encyclopedia of California Pottery.* Paducah, KY: Collector Books, 1992.

Chipman, Jack. *Collectors Encyclopedia of California Pottery Second Edition.* Paducah, KY: Collector, Books 1999.

Schneider, Mike. *California Potteries The Complete Book.* Atglen, Pennsylvania: Schiffer Publishing Ltd., 1995.